ALL ABOUT

SINGING

A FUN AND SIMPLE GUIDE TO LEARNING TO SING

SPECIAL CD INCLUDES OVER 70 TRACKS
FEATURING DOZENS OF GREAT SONGS!

T0082069

by Elaine Schmidt

Edited by J. Mark Baker

ISBN 978-1-4234-4693-4

HAL•LEONARD®
CORPORATION

7777 W. BLUEMOUND RD. P.O. BOX 13819 MILWAUKEE, WI 53213

Copyright © 2011 by HAL LEONARD CORPORATION
International Copyright Secured   All Rights Reserved

For all works contained herein:
Unauthorized copying, arranging, adapting, recording, Internet posting, public performance,
or other distribution of the printed or recorded music in this publication is an infringement of copyright.
Infringers are liable under the law.

Visit Hal Leonard Online at
www.halleonard.com

CONTENTS

Page   CD Track(s)

INTRODUCTION

ABOUT THIS BOOK

Singing is the most natural thing in the world. Young children sing freely, without a thought to whether it's easy or difficult. It's only once self-awareness begins to take over that we become embarrassed to have our singing voices heard.

Because singing is such a natural expression and activity for us, we can learn to sing in much less time that we can learn to play an instrument like the violin or guitar. But that doesn't mean it's a walk in the park. Singing takes concentration, hard work, diligence and discipline. In fact, singers and other musicians take offense if they're referred to as talented. Talented implies that the gift of singing fell from the sky and they happened to pick it up. A singer may have a nice voice or may be innately quite musical, but singing well is hard work.

The voice is a much more personal instrument than one you pack up in a case when your're done using it or, in the case of a piano or organ, one you leave in the concert hall when you're done performing. Your voice is always with you. It's yours alone, and it's completely unique in the world.

Your voice is also far more fragile than you might think. It's easy to injure a voice through bad singing habits and bad lifestyle choices. If you drop a trumpet on the ground, you can have the dents pounded out of it and keep playing. But if you injure your voice, you may change the way you sound forever. So pay close attention to your warm-up, practice, and performance habits and be gentle to your voice in your off-hours. Your voice is irreplaceable.

As you make your way through this book, you will learn how the voice works and how to use it well. You'll learn to read music, a skill that is imperative to the process of making your own, personal musical statements. If you have to rely on hearing other singers in order to learn new music, you'll end up learning their interpretations as well as the notes. Reading music frees you from relying on that crutch and allows you to read and understand what the songwriter put on paper for you to interpret. However, this book and CD are set up so that you can take full advantage of all music included, no matter what your level of music reading skill. This book will also help you select music that suits your voice and personal style. As you learn to sing, you'll come to appreciate the time, effort, and art that go into good singing. Have fun!

ABOUT THE CD

On the accompanying CD, you'll find demonstrations of the vocal warm-ups and many of the songs in this book. The included songs feature a full performance, as well as a "piano only" track for you to practice on your own. The CD should not be used as a substitute for learning to read music. Listening and reading should go together. Section 6 of the book is especially useful in helping you develop your music reading skills. Study it carefully.

ICON LEGEND

Included in every *All About* book are several icons to help you on your way. Keep an eye out for these.

AUDIO

This icon indicates a related track on the accompanying CD.

TRY THIS

Included with this icon are various bits of helpful advice about singing.

EXTRAS

This includes additional information on various topics that may be interesting and useful, but not necessarily essential.

DON'T FORGET

There's a lot of information in this book that may be difficult to remember. This refresher will help you stay the course.

DANGER!

Here, you'll learn how to avoid injury and keep your equipment from going on the fritz.

ORIGINS

Interesting little historical blurbs are included for fun and background information.

NUTS & BOLTS

Included with this last icon are tidbits on the fundamentals or building blocks of music.

Essentials

CHAPTER 1
FINDING YOUR VOICE

What's Ahead:
- Voice types
- Discovering your vocal range
- Trying out a song

Think of your friends and family and the fact that each of them has a speaking voice that's uniquely theirs. Most of us know these familiar voices immediately when we hear them. Singing voices are no different. Every singing voice on this planet is unique, thanks to the combination of *timbre* (tone quality), *pitch* (whether a voice is high or low), any sort of regional accent, and what sort of treatment the voice has gotten over the years. Like your height, the timbre, or sound, many of the qualities of your voice were decided for you before you were born. Someone born with a tenor voice can no more become a bass than a short person can become tall.

Some of the factors that make your voice unique are environmental rather than genetic. Too many years of smoking or a tendency to scream at sporting events or rock concerts can have a huge impact on a voice. Although some aspects of your voice are determined for you, there are things you can change. You can refine the sound you make by learning to sing and breathe naturally and correctly, you can protect it from damage, and you can learn to control your voice and add expression and nuance to it. With careful work you can even expand the range a bit to reach a few higher or lower notes. You noticed the word "work" in that last sentence, did you? Singing is work. It may look like effortless fun to stand onstage and sing, and it should look that way to the audience, but building a lasting career as a singer takes years of hard work. Singers must learn the discipline of practice as well as the discipline of treating their voice well when they're not singing.

VOICE TYPES

Distinct though they may be, most singing voices fall into one of six broad range categories: soprano, mezzo-soprano, alto, tenor, baritone, or bass. Sopranos are the highest of the female voice while tenors are the highest of the male voices. Mezzo-sopranos and baritones are somewhat lower voices, while altos and basses are the lowest. Although these categories are traditionally used in classical and choral music, they're useful in any style of singing. Pop/rock singer Peter Cetera, opera singer Placido Domingo, and jazz singer Mel Torme are all tenors, wildly different musicians, but all tenors.

There are very few basses in the world of rock and roll. One of the most distinctive is Brad Roberts, lead singer of the Canadian band Crash Test Dummies. His deep voice made international hits of songs like "Superman's Song" and "Mmm Mmm Mmm Mmm." Even rarer are the high "whistle" tones sung by Mariah Carey in songs like "Emotions."

DISCOVERING YOUR VOCAL RANGE

Step one in learning to sing is finding out what voice type you are, which means finding out how high and low you can comfortably sing. If you have sung in a chorus or have sung some solos in the past, you may already know your voice type. If you do, skip to the music at the end of this chapter and sing the version appropriate for your voice type. Even if you've sung in the past, confirming your voice type may be helpful to make sure you're singing music suited to your voice.

The first tracks on the CD that accompanies this book are designed to help you find your own voice range. Track 1 (women's voices) and Track 2 (men's voices) will present an exercise in matching pitches to get you started. The singers will sing several pitches, repeating each one several times. Your task is to listen carefully to the pitch and then match it, singing the same pitch along with the singer. The singers will present several pitches in two octaves, essentially higher or lower versions of the same note, so that you become accustomed to hearing octaves.

Pay close attention to the octaves. Musical notes are organized into eight-note scales that use the letters A through G for their names. Each scale begins and ends on notes of the same name, which are an octave apart. Make sure you are not only matching the pitch of a note, but also the octave. To help you hear and understand octaves, try singing the note you're matching in its higher or lower version.

Once you're comfortable matching pitches with the singers on the CD, listen to Track 3 (women) and Track 4 (men). You will hear the singers presenting scales, slowly. In each case, they will sustain the beginning note of the scale for you to match before they begin. Sing along with the scales several times, going as high or low as is comfortable for your voice. The following examples will give you the actual notes of the scales the singers are singing on the CD.

For women:

For men:

Even if you don't read music, you can use the printed scales as a roadmap to your own range. Begin by pointing with a pencil to the first note of the scale you're about to sing. Point to each note as you sing it. When you come to the point where you can no longer comfortably sing the next note, circle the last note you sang. Sing the scales with the CD several times. As you get warmed up, you may find that you can sing a few notes higher or lower than you did on your first try.

Now that you've marked your range on the printed scales, compare them to the ranges listed below. Pick the range that matches your own range most closely. Don't worry if your range doesn't match exactly with the ranges printed; just pick the one closest to your own.

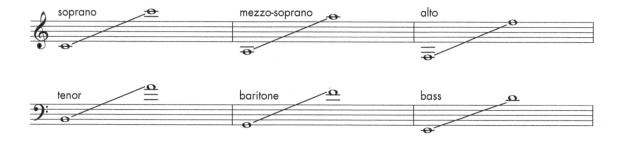

Your voice range will almost certainly expand as you begin singing and practicing regularly. Singing is like participating in a sport in that you always want to warm up and flex your muscles before you begin, and the more you sing and use your voice correctly, the better and stronger it will get. For starters, however, having an idea of what type of voice you have will help you pick music that suits your voice.

If you know you're soprano, don't choose music written for a low voice. If you're a bass, don't select songs written for high, tenor voices. If you want to sing songs that were written for a voice that is higher or lower than your own, you can always sing a version that has been *transposed* for your voice type. Transposing means moving the song and its accompaniment to a higher or lower key. Many songs are printed in both "high voice" and "low voice" editions.

TRYING OUT A SONG

It's time to try a song. Listen to the singer on Track 5 and 6 as she sings the high voice and low voice versions of the African-American spiritual, "Sometimes I Feel Like a Motherless Child."

After you've listened to the song a few times, choose your voice part and sing along. If you find the song too high or too low, don't be afraid to try the higher or lower version.

Don't worry if you don't know how to read music yet—this song is straightforward enough that you should be able to pick up the song after hearing it a few times. We'll deal with reading music later in the book. Although some singers never learn to read music, it's worth taking the time to learn. Reading music allows you to make your own interpretations of songs, instead of learning someone else's interpretation as you listen to their recordings to learn your songs. Reading music also frees you from having to rely heavily on accompanists as you're learning songs.

Sometimes I Feel Like a Motherless Child

CHAPTER 2
HOW THE VOICE WORKS

What's Ahead:
- The vocal cords
- The break
- Take a deep breath
- Support

THE VOCAL CORDS

Now that you know what type of voice you have, it's time to lean how your body is going about producing a singing sound. The human voice is really an amazing little machine. Although we like to refer to them as *vocal cords*, the two little membranes that vibrate against one another to produce vocal sound are actually folded mucous membranes. They are correctly known as *vocal folds*. Those folds are pulled taut across the larynx to produce speaking or singing sounds, but they move aside to allow us to breathe and swallow.

Everything you eat, drink, or inhale affects your vocal folds. Drinking a nice cold glass of milk will leave a film of milk on your vocal folds that can give you a sort of murky sound if you sing shortly afterward. Drinking hard liquor can dry out your vocal folds and give them a rough, raspy sound. Salty foods can cause them to swell. Basically, you sing what you eat and drink.

These little vocal folds vibrate at an incredible rate of speed to produce notes. When you hear a musician talking about an "A-440," they're referring to the A above middle C, which falls in the soprano, mezzo-soprano, alto, and tenor ranges. It's called "A-440" because it takes 440 vibrations per second to produce that pitch. That's right, if you sing that note, your vocal folds are vibrating 440 times per second. Higher notes require more vibrations per second. Lower notes require fewer vibrations per second. You might think that fewer vibrations per second would be easier to accomplish and therefore we should all relax and sing in the lower alto or bass ranges. But it doesn't work that way. As we discussed in the last chapter, your voice type was largely decided for you by genetics.

Vocal Folds Opened

Vocal Folds Closed

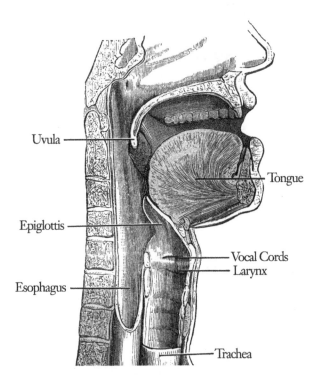

Uvula

Tongue

Epiglottis

Vocal Cords
Larynx

Esophagus

Trachea

Although the vocal folds are the only parts of the body that produce vocal sound, most singers can produce different kinds of sound by allowing that sound to resonate differently in the body. There are two main types of vocal production, known as *chest voice* and *head voice.*

Chest voice and head voice are the lower and higher portions of a singer's range. In the lower part of your range you can sing in a style that is close to loud speaking. It's called chest voice because your chest resonates as you produce notes in this range. In fact, if you place your hand on the upper part of your chest and sing some of the lower notes in your range, you'll be able to feel the vibrations with your hand.

Although all singers can use head and chest voices, regardless of whether they're sopranos, basses, or something in between, there are some voice types that use one or the other most frequently. Head voice is the sound that a woman will make when singing her high notes. The sound fills the sinus cavities, resonating in the mask of the face.

Listen to the singers on Tracks 7 and 8 as they begin singing in *chest voice* and move into the higher *head voice* area of their ranges.

Both men and women can sing with a chest voice or head voice. Some men can produce an additional sound called *falsetto*, or false voice. The sound, which is actually a type of head voice, is high and sounds quite a bit like a female voice, although it's usually more strident than a woman's voice would be. The "Broadway belt," a loud, almost shouting style of singing popular on the musical theater stage, is a type of chest voice.

Let's see if you can locate your own chest voice. Start with a note that's low in your range, but too low to be comfortable to sing with a full sound. Place your hand on your chest to feel the chest voice resonance. Moving upward in pitch, just as the singers did on Tracks 7 and 8, sing a smooth scale, connecting the notes as through you're actually singing a song.

THE BREAK

All singers can produce chest voice and head voice sounds. Most singers experience sort of a vocal tripwire between the two types of singing, called *the break.* You'll know your break when you encounter it—it sounds a bit like an adolescent boy's voice breaking as it begins changing. It's a natural phenomenon—every voice has one—but it's not the show-stopping obstacle you might think. For some singers, the sound difference between head and chest voice is quite distinct, for others not so much.

Listen to the singers in Tracks 7 and 8 again, as they sing over their breaks. Imitate what they're doing, starting low in your range with your hand on your chest to feel the vibrations of chest voice singing and moving up the scale until your voice flips into head voice. You will feel and hear the difference instantly. There is no magic pill to make the break disappear. You simply have to know that it exists and practice making a smooth transition over the break whenever a song requires that you move from chest voice to head voice. Sing along with the singers in this example and try smoothing over your own break.

To understand falsetto, listen to the singer in Track 8 as he moves into his falsetto range. Men, feel free to sing along with this example and see if you too can produce a high, falsetto sound.

All singers have to decide how to handle their break. Without a vocal break in their voices, yodelers wouldn't be able to make their trademark sound and singers like Patsy Cline and Buddy Holly would have been pretty bland. But not every song or style of music requires an obvious break in the voice. In fact, most don't.

TAKE A DEEP BREATH

Relaxing and supporting your sound with air will make an enormous difference in smoothing over the break in your voice. Don't force—don't blast air through your throat to make sound in any part of your register. Understand exactly where your own break lies and use steady, even support and a relaxed throat and jaw as you approach it.

Whenever your break presents a problem in a song, do just what the singers did on the recording. Begin a few notes above or below your break and sing over the break, always working for a smooth transition. Remember, natural, relaxed singing and lots of steady air will make an enormous difference.

Resonance, whether it's primarily in the head or chest of the singer, is essential to singing. Try singing a note—any note—and then pinching your nose shut as you hold the note. The result is a sound that's as pinched as your nose is at the moment.

We've all heard someone singing and trying to be funny. It almost always involved a painfully tight, pinched sound that anyone can immediately tell is just plain bad. The actor Don Knotts did a fine job of that kind of singing whenever his Barney Fife character had to sing on the old Andy Griffith show. Those episodes still come up in reruns today and his singing remains hilarious, more than 40 years after it was put on film. The thing that made his singing funny was that it obviously was not a natural sound.

Everyone who speaks does so with their own natural sound. You can alter your speaking voice to be nasal, gravely, or whiney, but you can't sustain that for very long without feeling your throat becoming tired. Singing works exactly the same way. A natural singing sound is one that's relaxed and is both easy and comfortable to produce. If you're tightening up your throat, your abdominal muscles, your jaw, or any other part of your body in order to sing, you're not producing a natural sound.

Listen to Tracks 9 and 10, the American spiritual, "Amazing Grace." Sing along with the singer, in either the low or high voice version of the song, and think about keeping every part of your body relaxed as you sing.

Amazing Grace

Copyright © 2000 by HAL LEONARD CORPORATION
International Copyright Secured All Rights Reserved

Words by JOHN NEWTON
Traditional American Melody
from Carrell and Clayton's *Virginia Harmony*

There are lots of ways to produce a tight, inflexible vocal sound. The tongue, if it's too high and rigid, or pulled too far back in the mouth, can create tension. The jaw, if it's clamped, pushed out or down can also create terrible tension. Shallow breathing can also create damaging tension. Even a singer's lips, if they're tight or rigid, can cause tension that restricts the sound.

A good way to check for unwanted tension is to sing a long, relaxed note during your warm-up or practice session and move, one at a time, your tongue, jaw, and lips freely. You are going to look silly, so you may want to move away from the window. You'll also sound a little silly, so don't expect to impress anyone with this exercise.

SUPPORT

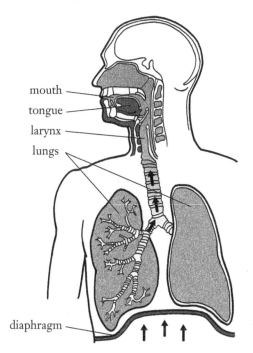

mouth
tongue
larynx
lungs

diaphragm

A lovely set of vocal folds that can produce a sweet or big sound is only half of the equation that adds up to good singing. The other half is *support*, the steady, efficient manner in which a singer uses air. The little powerhouse that supports your singing voice, and actually allows you take a lifetime of breaths, is a sheet of muscle at the bottom of the ribcage known as the *diaphragm*. It's this muscle that allows us to inhale and exhale and to control our breathing so that we can sing or play wind and brass instruments like the flute or trumpet.

To feel your diaphragm at work, stand up straight and place your hand on your abdomen, covering your navel. Take a medium-sized breath and give a loud, short shout on the word "Ha!" You've probably noticed your diaphragm before, perhaps if you've laughed too hard and too long. That ache in your stomach was actually your diaphragm objecting to the overuse.

try this

Lie down on the floor, with your legs stretched out, flat on the floor. Place your hands on your abdomen, one in the region above your navel and one in the region below your navel. Take a few deep, relaxing breaths and feel the diaphragm at work. If you can't feel the diaphragm working, try the "Ha!" exercise again to locate the muscle and then redo the deep breathing.

When singers talk about singing from the diaphragm, or supporting their sound, they are referring to taking deep, relaxed breaths, just as you did while sprawled out on the floor. The following exercise will help you remember to use your diaphragm as you breathe to sing. This is a good exercise to use to start your daily practice.

Stand up straight, with one hand on your chest and the other on your navel. Let out the air in your lungs. Refill your lungs by taking a high, shallow breath. You should feel your chest rise and your ribcage expand a bit.

Now let out most of that breath, keeping your chest high and your rib cage expanded. Inhale again, deeply this time, letting the air flow deep into your lungs. You will feel your stomach expand with the breath. If it's not working for you, keep your hands in place and try panting like a puppy. This helps get the diaphragm moving. Remember, when we do most tasks in our daily lives, like working at a computer or driving a car, we are usually slouching and are rarely taking deep relaxing breaths. Try the deep breath again. It should feel easier, more relaxed than the high, shallow breath. The reason for the difference in feeling is that the high breath requires you to move the bone and cartilage of your rib cage. Those are slow-moving vehicles! When you breathe deeply, using your diaphragm, you are moving only soft tissue, which is much easier to accomplish.

Keeping your rib cage expanded and your chest high as you sing allows you to make the most of your lung capacity without having to raise and lower those structural elements each time you breathe. It also allows you to make good use of that resonating space. Later in the book you'll learn some exercises that will help you learn to use the diaphragm more efficiently.

Thinking about what you've learned about the voice and diaphragm, listen to the singer on Tracks 9 and 10 sing "Amazing Grace." Sing along, with one hand on your chest and the other on your abdomen. Keep your chest high and expanded as you take deep, relaxed breaths to sustain this lovely melody. Try to breathe only where the singer on the CD breathes. If you can't manage the long lines just yet, take smaller breaths along the way. Don't keep singing until you haven't got any air left to give. If you do, you'll create tension and noise as you gulp air at the end of a phrase.

> When you inhale to sing, don't fill up and then hold your breath until it's time to start singing. Time your breath carefully so that you finish inhaling just before you have to sing. This way, you get the most out of that lungful of air—and you stay relaxed.

If you're having trouble getting through the long lines of "Amazing Grace," sing it without the recording at a slightly faster *tempo* (speed). Over the course of several days, work on slowing it down without adding extra breaths. Each time you take it a notch slower, you're asking your lungs to go a little longer before taking another breath. This is a good way to expand your lung capacity and breath control

Once you have gotten comfortable sustaining the long lines of this piece, go to Track 11, a slower version of the same song. Sing along again. You will notice that the song is a little slower in this track than it was the first time you sang it. That means that you will have to sustain slightly longer lines—so make sure you take deep, relaxed breaths. Again, this may take a few days of practice, but keep at it and you'll see a difference very quickly.

One more time... let's slow the piece down. Sing along with Track 12 and see if you can sustain the long lines. If not, you know what to do: practice singing the piece without the recording, taking care to take in lots of air.

You may have noticed a pattern here: you have been working on a small issue, sustaining the long lines of "Amazing Grace" at slower and slower tempos over the course of several days, making steady gradual progress toward your goal. Welcome to the world of practicing music. From beginners with a book in hand to professionals who tour the world, this is how musicians practice.

Getting to Work

CHAPTER 3
BREATHING AND POSTURE

What's Ahead:

- Assume the position
- Daily breathing exercise
- Mother always said, "Stand up straight."
- Give me some air

Creating a full, free, natural sound is a full-body endeavor. Although your vocal folds reside in your throat, everything from your sinuses to your feet is involved when you begin to sing. Whether you're standing in front of an audience or sitting in a choir rehearsal, your posture and body position have an enormous effect on the sound you produce.

try this

> We've talked a little bit about breathing already, but it's time to dig a little deeper. For an object lesson on the importance of posture and body position, stand up, put your feet close together and slouch forward as much as your body will let you. Now, without straightening up at all, try taking a deep breath and singing a lovely resonant note. It didn't work well, did it? Try doing the same thing while slumped in a chair. Even worse!

ASSUME THE POSITION

Breathing correctly is the key to good singing, but good posture is the key to good breathing. When we stand to sing, we plant our feet at about shoulder width and center our body weight, and our shoulders and hips. There will be situations, like choir rehearsals, where you're going to find yourself singing while seated. Although you can't center your hips and shoulders above your feet while seated in a chair, you can still use good posture. When singing from a seated position, always sit up straight, with both feet flat on the floor.

danger

> Crossing your legs pulls your spine out of alignment and tugs at the muscles of your back and abdomen—none of which makes for good breathing.

When sitting to sing, you want to sit with your spine straight and your back only lightly touching the back of the chair. If your spine is curved forward, your lungs and diaphragm are compressed and you can't possibly get a good, deep breath. Curving your spine in the opposite direction creates muscle tension. Leaning your weight on the back of the chair stops your lungs from expanding completely when you breathe. The solution is to sit up straight, use the back of the chair for a little support and breathe deeply. Every now and then (when you're not singing, please!), you can roll from hip to hip in the chair—a little like doing a warm-up for a balancing ball workout. As you roll onto your right hip, bring your right shoulder down toward your hip and raise your left shoulder. Repeat on the opposite side. This will help keep your muscles from getting tense during a long rehearsal. If you are able to stand as you practice, do so. If not, be extra aware of posture and breathing as you sit.

When you're standing and singing, make sure you don't lock your knees. Locking your knees changes blood flow in your legs and can cause you to get light-headed or even to faint. Keep your knees straight, but not locked in position.

With your feet planted and knees unlocked, bend forward to touch your toes. Relax. Now pull up into a standing position, imagining that you are moving up one vertebra at a time. Once you're upright again, imagine a string attached to the top of our head, pulling you upright.

Now that the framework is in place, let's get your lungs and diaphragm involved. Exhale as much air as you can comfortably manage. Now, take in three relaxed, deep breaths, trying to fill your lungs in thirds. Each of the three breaths should make your lungs feel fuller, with the last one really topping things off. Now, before you exhale, take two little sniffs of air through your nose, paying attention to the feeling of expansion in your chest and abdomen. Let the air out in a long, even hiss.

Remember, this position is all about being upright and relaxed. Take care not to slump forward, since this will seriously limit the amount of air you can take in. Also, be careful not to push your shoulders too far back, since this will cause tension that will hinder good breathing.

Once you're in the position described above, raise your chest so that your rib cage is open and expanded. As you breathe, keep your rib cage in this position, letting your diaphragm and the muscles of your abdomen do the heavy lifting for you. If your chest is rising and falling as you breathe, you're wasting energy and creating tension.

DAILY BREATHING EXERCISE

Breathing while standing in your singing stance may also feel a bit odd at first. Your lungs, which are accustomed to being crunched for space while you're slouching, are going to feel exceptionally full when you start breathing deeply in this posture.

Assume your relaxed-but-upright singing posture. Pick a note that's comfortable for you to sing and sustain. Exhale. Inhale slowly and steadily for four counts and immediately begin sustaining the note you chose, at a medium volume. Stay relaxed and sustain that note as long as you comfortably can, trying to maintain a steady sound free of bumps or dips. Repeat the exercise, sustaining the note at a louder volume, still striving for a steady, smooth sound.

Try the same exercise from a seated position, always being aware of posture and relaxed, deep breathing. In addition to being great as part of a singing warm-up, these breathing exercises are wonderful, quick stress relievers at anytime of the day. A little deep breathing at the office may help get you through a tough day at work.

 If you feel yourself tensing up during these exercises, repeat the toe-touching exercise above to relax. If you're seated, use the hip-rolling exercise.

Repeat the exercise again, this time using a softer volume, again striving for a smooth, steady sound. It's a good idea to try this exercise while seated, maintaining good posture. This is a good daily exercise for relaxing, whether you're about to warm up and practice, sing a concert, or step into a high-pressure meeting at work. After a week or two of doing this exercise every day, you should notice that the notes you're sustaining are getting smoother and stronger. You'll also notice that you sustain them longer.

When you start noticing an improvement, try adding one more repeat of the exercise to your routine—this one at the softest volume you can possibly produce. This addition will help you learn to control your voice and the air you use to support it.

MOTHER ALWAYS SAID, "STAND UP STRAIGHT."

Good posture doesn't mean a rigid, uncomfortable stance. The military "at attention" sort of posture is good for nothing except standing at attention in the military. Think of good posture more in "at ease" terms. Good posture is relaxed posture, with the shoulders and hips centered over the feet and the muscles relaxed enough to allow fluid, smooth movement. Keeping the rib cage high (another way to think about not slouching) and keeping the head balanced easily on the shoulders leaves the muscles of the back and shoulders loose and comfortable. The effect of good posture on the way your back and shoulders feel is tremendous, but the effect of good posture on the way you look is even greater. A person standing well looks assured, relaxed, and alert. Someone slouching or hunched looks harried, tired, and uncertain. Pay attention to people around you for a few days and you'll notice that standing and sitting with good posture even makes a person's clothing look nicer.

Good posture is not a sometimes proposition. Your muscles have memory. If you get in the habit of slouching or sitting up straight, your muscles will want to pull you into that position every time you're seated. The same is true for your standing posture. Therefore, if you want your singing posture to be good, you're going to have to pay attention to your posture in everything you do, from driving your car to eating dinner and watching television.

Most of us are sloppy in our posture, as a rule. We slouch, with our spines curved like the letter C, our shoulders drooping forward, and our necks at an awkward angle. We sit like this in front of the computer, in front of the television, and while we drive our cars. As a result, a good singing posture can feel exaggerated and even a bit pretentious at first. Get over it. Standing up straight and staying relaxed is the only way to let your voice sound its best.

GIVE ME SOME AIR

Breathing while singing a song adds one more complicating factor to the process of taking in air: you have to maintain the rhythm and tempo of the music while still taking a breath. Beginning the song with a deep relaxed breath is essential as a starting point. Once the song has begun, however, you have to have a plan for breathing.

Most singers mark the spots in the music at which they plan to breathe, using a comma or a little letter V above the notes as their symbol. A comma in parentheses is often used to indicate an optional breath. Even if you're singing from a lyric sheet without a note of music in sight, marking breaths in this way is important. Mark every breath you plan to take, as well as the optional ones for moments when you may need them. Then practice them. Every time you sing the song, take the breaths exactly as you've marked them. The breathing will become as much a part of the song as the notes and lyrics, which will ensure that you won't space out, forget to breathe, and run amuck onstage.

In order to catch a breath between phrases without making the next entrance late, you have to rob the last note of the phrase that's ending, catch a quick, deep, relaxed breath and come in on time with the next phrase. You can use this technique of robbing one note to secure an entrance in your warm-up exercises to get comfortable with the technique.

Breathing while singing is a lot like breathing while reading aloud. You don't want to slice up a word in order to breathe, nor do you want to carve up a sentence or catch a breath. The punctuation in the lyrics can often make your breathing decisions for you. Still, there will be times when a breath has to be taken and there's not an obvious place to do it. In that case, try several different spots until you find the one that is the least disruptive to the music.

Do the breathing and posture exercises above and then sing the following English song, "O Waly, Waly," which is also known as "The Water Is Wide." A favorite of recitalists, this song is a gentle, plaintive melody that requires even, effortless support.

O Waly, Waly
(The Water Is Wide)

Copyright © 2000 by HAL LEONARD CORPORATION
International Copyright Secured   All Rights Reserved

English Folksong

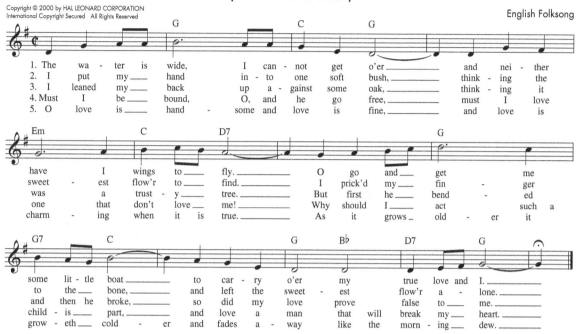

If you can accompany yourself on piano or guitar, or have an accompanist or a karaoke track to work with, you may enjoy trying your hand at the following World War II-era pop song, "I'll Be Home for Christmas," by Kim Gannon and Walter Kent. The lyrical lines of the song require smooth, even support and smooth, seamless breathing. Look for recordings by Bing Crosby or Frank Sinatra and more recent recordings by Kristin Chenoweth or Sarah McLachlan.

I'll Be Home for Christmas

Words and Music by KIM GANNON
and WALTER KENT

© Copyright 1943 by Gannon & Kent Music Co., Inc., Beverly Hills, CA
Copyright Renewed
International Copyright Secured   All Rights Reserved

You're not the only one who needs to know where you're going to breathe. Your accompanist will be able to support your phrasing if he or she knows where you're going to take breaths. Pencil breath marks in his or her part as well. Many accompanists take breaths with the singer whenever they're marked—to help create a tighter ensemble.

The other breathing issue for singers is catching breaths quickly in fast pieces of music. To avoid tension and to get as much air in as possible in a short bit of time, open your throat as though you're yawning as you inhale. This gives you a wide-open airway and cuts down on the noise that occurs when you inhale too quickly with a tight throat.

The following song, "Rockin' Robin," was written by Leon René under the pen name "Jimmie Thomas." Check out recordings by Bobby Day, who first made it a hit in 1958, or the Jackson 5. Listen to the accompaniment on Track 15 and try it yourself. Remember to relax as you take those quick breaths.

Rockin' Robin

Words and Music by
J. THOMAS

Copyright © 2005 by HAL LEONARD CORPORATION
International Copyright Secured   All Rights Reserved

Practice your breaths as though they are part of the song, so that the breaths become part of the music and lyrics. That way, you'll never forget to breathe and risk running out of air in the middle of a phrase.

Congratulations! You have just learned your first warm-up exercises. These little breathing exercises are a good start to any practice session as well as a good warm-up before a performance. They will help you get your body ready to sing your best.

You're not just full of hot air. Hold your hand about six inches directly in front of your mouth. Blow like you are trying to steam up a mirror or moistening your glasses before cleaning them. Notice the warmth of the air you're releasing.

Now put your hand back in that same position and blow as though you are putting out a candle or cooling a hot bite of food. Notice the coolness of the air you're releasing.

As you're singing, pay attention to the temperature of the air you're releasing. You may find it helpful to experiment with warming up your stream of air or cooling it down to create a slightly different vocal sound.

Here's a song—"My Heart Will Go On," from the film *Titanic*—that will help you work on breathing. Learn the song, singing counting syllables ("1&2&3&4&" etc.) and then singing note names. Then begin applying lyrics. If you learn it this way, by the time you begin worrying about the lyrics you'll be quite familiar with the song and will be able to devote your attention to the words. As you are first learning it, practice taking breaths during the rests, without coming in late on the next note.

My Heart Will Go On

(Love Theme from 'Titanic')

from the Paramount and Twentieth Century Fox Motion Picture TITANIC

Music by JAMES HORNER
Lyric by WILL JENNINGS

Copyright © 1997 Sony/ATV Music Publishing LLC, T C F Music Publishing, Inc., Fox Film Music Corporation and Blue Sky Rider Songs
All Rights on behalf of Sony/ATV Music Publishing LLC Administered by Sony/ATV Music Publishing LLC, 8 Music Square West, Nashville, TN 37203
All Rights on behalf of Blue Sky Rider Songs Administered by Irving Music, Inc.
International Copyright Secured   All Rights Reserved

CHAPTER 4
DAILY WARM-UP AND PRACTICE

What's Ahead:
- Learning to practice
- Focus
- Body warm-up
- Vocal warm-up

LEARNING TO PRACTICE

Learning to sing means learning to practice. Practicing is more than just learning the song or songs you plan to sing at an upcoming event. It's a day-by-day process of learning to create a natural, relaxed sound that's as consistent as possible from the top to the bottom of your range. It also means learning to control your voice the same way a violinist or trumpeter learns to control their instrument. The voice is an instrument—one that you carry with you at all times. If you don't practice and perfect your voice, all of your song interpretations will be determined by what you can manage to make your voice do on any given day rather than by what you really want to do with it.

Instrumentalists spend practice time working on scales and exercises to develop technical skills that allow them to play fast passages cleanly, sustain long notes with an even, controlled sound and other skills. Singers do exactly the same thing in their practice. Singers also work on developing good singing habits so that they will be able to sing for many years to come without doing damage to their voices. Essentially, practicing is the hard work that makes performance sound effortless. You may have the sort of naturally lovely voice that has people telling you that you should be singing, but without practicing, those comments will be the extent of your musical career. A lovely voice is a gift—the ability to sing expressively and impressively is the result of practice.

One of the first challenges of adding practice sessions to daily schedule is finding a place to practice. In order to practice well, you need to find a quiet space where you cannot be clearly heard by others. If you're practicing in the dining room while your family is watching television in the living room, you're going to be inhibited by the fact that they can hear every note you sing and you'll feel the need to sing quietly so they can enjoy their program. Likewise, practicing isn't something you can accomplish in the restroom at work during lunch. You need to find a place where you are isolated enough to sing without worrying what others might think of your practice routine and feel free to sing with a full, relaxed voice. Some people are able to find time alone at home for practice, others arrange for time at a local church. Teachers can often find time in their classrooms at the end of the day, when the majority of the staff has gone home. Some singers, and other musicians, build reasonably soundproof areas in their basements or garages. Others rent a little practice room, or studio, at a local musical school or music store. These little rooms are often pretty dingy, but they usually rent by the half-hour on a set, weekly schedule. The disadvantage to renting space is that it costs money—the advantage is that if you're paying for the time in a practice room you'll probably work hard while you're there in order to justify the cost. Wherever you go to practice, you need to be comfortable singing freely in the space.

Once you have a space set up for yourself, you need to set up a routine that you will follow in each practice session. Singing is a little like a sport since singers, both professionals and amateurs, and athletes have to warm up before practicing or performing in order to avoid injuries. Singing is nothing like a sport however, in terms of effort and exertion. When you're running a marathon, go right ahead and "push through the pain." Athletics are all about exerting yourself and pushing yourself to new levels of endurance and accomplishment. Singing with that mentality will end your career before it starts. Remember, many of the qualities of your voice were determined before you knew how to speak. You can work, gently, to expand your range a bit and to polish your technical skills, but unless you're singing with a relaxed sound that's natural to your voice, you won't be singing for long.

If singing causes pain—stop! See a voice teacher or coach for an opinion on what's wrong and don't be surprised if they recommend that you see a throat specialist. But don't assume that you'll feel pain if you're doing damage to your voice. For singers, career-ending injuries can be sneaky. What starts as a little difficulty hitting a high note can turn into seriously damaged vocal cords without the singer knowing it. There's often no pain involved, so singers have to rely on the way they sound and the way they feel as they sing.

The good news, at least time-wise, is that singers can't train for the long hours required of athletes, or practice the long hours that many instrumentalists do without causing terrible wear and tear on their throats. Practice room time is precious, so every note of the warm-up and practice session has to be put to good use. It's best to begin every practice session with the same warm-up, and to use that same warm-up as you get ready for a performance. The warm-up is a way to center your thoughts on your singing and to relax, listen to yourself and sing well. Warm-ups don't take a lot of time, but they can make a world of difference in the way you sound when you sing and the way you feel when you step out in front of your audience.

Singers should practice for regular, relatively short periods every day or every other day, and should always follow a routine that allows time to warm up and flex the body and voice before diving into work.

A healthy practice routine should consist of the following steps: focus, body warm-up, and vocal warm-up.

FOCUS

Take a few minutes to clear your head. Let go of the mountain of things we all have to deal with in any given day and focus your mind on the fact that you're about to sing. Imagine picking up the various things that are occupying your thoughts and putting them on a shelf where you can pick them up later, after your practice session is over. Once you get used to focusing intently on your singing, it will become a welcome half-hour or hour vacation from the cares and mental lists you usually carry around. This is one of the great joys of singing.

BODY WARM-UP

Take a deep relaxing breath and let it out slowly.

Bend at the waist to touch your toes and pull yourself up slowly, as though moving one vertebra at a time.

Take a deep relaxing breath and let it out slowly.

Letting your arms and hands hang loose at your sides, shake them about. Let your arms and hands flop limply as you shake your arms.

Take a deep relaxing breath and let it out slowly.

The shoulders seem to be the first muscles in the body to respond to stress and tension. Slowly, gently, roll your shoulders to relax those muscles.

If your shoulders are particularly tight, you can cross one arm to the opposite shoulder and rest the fingers on the spot the feels the most tense.

Angle your head slightly toward the opposite shoulder until you feel a slight pull in the muscles under your hand. Return your head slowly to an upright position and then repeat on the other shoulder.

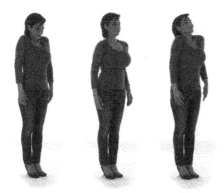

Take a deep relaxing breath and let it out slowly.

Roll your shoulders slowly, gracefully, and gently to help release the tension that remains.

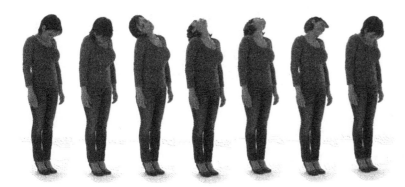

Take a deep relaxing breath and let it out slowly.

Move your head, slowly, from side to side and then, still slowly, drop your chin as close to your chest as you can. Beginning in this position, roll your head slowly and gently in a complete circle to the side, back and other side, until your chin is back in the starting position.

Take a deep relaxing breath and let it out slowly.

Keeping your neck and shoulders relaxed, smile broadly—until it feels completely silly.

Take a deep relaxing breath and let it out slowly.

Open your mouth widely, as you would at the dentist's office, and slowly let it close again.

Take a deep relaxing breath and let it out slowly.

The following exercise is meant to relax the muscles of the face and jaw. It should be done fluidly, moving from position to position as smoothly as possible.

1. Start by pushing your lips forward into an exaggerated "oo" (as in moon) position.

4. Move to an exaggerated "ay" (as in wait) position.

2. Move your lips slowly to an exaggerated "ee" (as in beet) position.

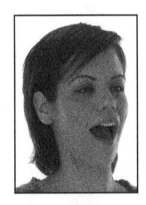

5. Move to an exaggerated "ah" (as in father) position.

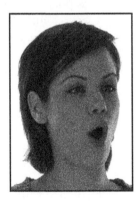

3. Drop your jaw and moving your lips to an "oh" (as in bowl) position.

Take a deep relaxing breath and let it out slowly.

VOCAL WARM-UP

Each warm-up exercise begins with an example of how it should sound. After the example, there is no singer, just the piano playing the exercise for you to sing. If the exercise gets too high or too low for you, if your throat feels tight, if you start straining, or if you can't hit the note, just stop and wait for the exercise to come into your range. After some work, you might be able to go higher or lower. Remember this: everyone's range is different. You might be an alto, so the high notes of a soprano are out of your reach, or you might be a tenor and therefore are unable to sing the low notes of a baritone. That's okay. Develop your voice to its unique potential.

Mee _____
Zee _____
Nee _____
See _____

This exercise is to be done slowly, at a moderately full (or *mezzo forte*) volume. Repeat this exercise with the following syllables: mee; may; mah; moe; moo. Then change the first consonant to: V; W; F; H; N; S; Th; R; J; L. The goal is to make your vowels warm and open, and to make your consonants clear, but not hard or disruptive, and to make the moves from one note to the next smooth and fluid.

Mee _____
Mah _____

Like the previous exercise, this one should be at a fairly quick tempo and a moderately full (or *mezzo forte*) volume. Repeat this exercise with the following syllables: mee; may; mah; moe; moo. Then change the first consonant to: V; W; F; H; N; S; Th; R; J; L. The goal is to make your vowels warm and open, and to make your consonants clear, but not hard or disruptive. Do a few of the syllables and a couple of the consonants each day, to avoid over-singing and to bring some variety to the warm-up each day.

Keeping a practice chart will allow you to see patterns and helps to keep days from slipping by with no practice. Record what time of day you practice, how long you practice, and what you work on.

CHAPTER 5
IT'S ALL ABOUT STYLE

What's Ahead:

- Copyrights and wrongs
- Listen up
- Rock/pop
- Country/western
- Blues
- Folk
- Celtic music

- Gospel
- R&B/Soul
- Broadway (musical theater)
- Jazz
- Classical
- Contemporary Christian
- World music

Music is like the ultimate buffet—it offers something for every imaginable taste. It's perfectly fine to have everything from country to opera and punk to jazz standards on your iPod, just don't expect to be able to sing all of those styles. You'll have to make some choices about the styles of music you're going to sing, based in large part on what sort of music suits your voice. You're not likely to sing a classical recital on a Friday and headline with a rock group on Saturday. But you can sing in related (or even unrelated) styles if you're careful with your voice.

COPYRIGHTS AND WRONGS

Before you do any buying, borrowing, or photocopying of music, or copying of recordings, you should know that laws exist to protect songwriters and recording artists from having their work duplicated without their permission—in other words, stolen.

As you begin singing gigs, you're going to expect to be paid for your efforts. Just as you deserve to be paid for your work, so do songwriters, lyricists, and recording artists. Copyrights are the rights of the creator or owner of a piece of "intellectual property" (songs, poems, books, plays, etc.) to make and distribute copies of their own work. The copyright symbol looks like this: ©

Printed music is most often copyrighted, as are books, poems, professional photographs, audio recordings, radio and television broadcasts, and motion pictures. Make sure you understand the copyright laws concerning the media you intend to copy before you find yourself in trouble. You cannot just photocopy music for yourself, your band, or accompanist. Breaking these laws can be quite expensive. For more detailed information, visit the Copyright Resource Center on the Music Publishers' Association website (http://mpa.org/).

LISTEN UP

There's no way to learn to sing in any given musical style other than to listen to the great singers of that style. In the following pages you'll find definitions of some of the major styles of music available to singers, and lists of some of the singers you might want to listen to in each style. The Internet has given aspiring singers of the current era a huge advantage over those who came before. If you want a little tasting of a singer's voice, go to Amazon.com, look them up, and you can listen to short excerpts of cuts from their albums. You can now also purchase single songs, without committing to an entire album, from many albums through Amazon and other online music shopping sites. YouTube is also a great resource for sampling various singers.

Some of the singers listed below are alive, kicking, and still recording. Others have retired and some have died. In all cases, their recordings live on.

ROCK/POP

Born in the early 1950s, rock and roll began with the likes of Bill Haley & His Comets and progressed through Elvis to groups like the Beatles, the Stones, and Queen, all of whom are now seen as "classic" rock. As the baby boom generation aged, their children played rock under the banner of "alternative." Sub-genres range from Detroit to Surf and from psychedelia to folk rock, hip hop, etc. Although there seems to be an endless public appetite for rock, it presents some serious issues for singers.

The first issue is learning to sing rock without damaging one's voice. Listen to some of the older rock singers that are still working, and compare their sound today to their sound on old recordings. The voices of some of these singers have taken a pounding over the years. The results can be heard in ranges that have narrowed over time and in a permanent gravelly sound. Some rock singers, like singer/songwriter James Taylor, decided mid-career to take voice lessons to protect their voices.

The other danger, and it may the greater danger, is hearing loss. In the early years of rock and roll, very few people thought about protecting their hearing from the music they were playing. Today, most rock musicians wear hearing protection of some sort onstage. Some wear earpieces that are miniature monitors, providing the bands sound at a controlled volume. Others wear what are known as "musicians' earplugs." These are actually sound filters that are fitted to a musician's ears just as a hearing aid would be. Interchangeable filters allow the musician to effectively turn the volume up and down. Protect your hearing! Once it's gone, it's gone forever.

The appealing thing about singing rock and pop is that it's not limited to any one type of voice. Singers include: James Taylor; Freddie Mercury (Queen); John Lennon and Paul McCartney (The Beatles); Kid Rock; Pat Benatar; Jackson Brown; Stevie Nicks (Fleetwood Mac); Eric Clapton; Darius Rucker (Hootie and the Blowfish); Bare Naked Ladies.

COUNTRY/WESTERN

Before World War II, Country music was a genre popular in the southern states of the U.S. and Western music had a following in the southwestern states. Then came the war. Servicemen, their families, and those looking for jobs moved across the country in an unprecedented migration, taking their music with them. When the war ended, many of those folks stayed where they had landed. Those who went back home took with them tastes and sounds of far-flung corners of the country. This was the point at which Country and Western music began to merge, and the point at which both genres developed a following across the country. Today you're as likely to hear Country music in Minnesota as in Georgia.

Country music grew out of the traditions and roots of folks in the South, blending blues with Celtic music and folk tunes with blues melodies and harmonies. The result was called "Hillbilly" music until after World War II.

Western music was an equally curious mix of the folk music brought to the region by settlers from the East and from Europe with the ethnic music of Mexico.

Country/western styles range from honky-tonk to rockabilly and from Bakersfield to bluegrass. Before World War II and before the rock and roll explosion of the early 1950s, country and western singers were pretty well doomed to a career in obscurity, at least from a national perspective. But in the wake of mega stars like Elvis and Garth Brooks, both of whom started out in Country music, the sky's the limit.

Country greats: Patsy Cline; Garth Brooks; Chet Atkins; Dolly Parton.

BLUES

"You can't sing the blues 'til you've paid your dues," goes a saying famous among jazz and blues musicians. The Blues are just what the name implies: sad tunes. The genre, which grew out of the intolerable conditions that enslaved Africans were forced into in the American South, is a mix of elements of the spirituals, work songs and other musical forms of the South's African population, framed by the tradition of English and Celtic ballads common among the white population of the South. Blues styles vary from locale to locale, sporting names like Mississippi blues, Chicago blues and swamp blues. The blues are built of repetitive patters, usually in lengths of eight or twelve bars.

Although singing the blues requires a care-worn voice and to-the-bone understanding of the style, singing derivatives of the blues, like rockabilly, might be an easier task.

Blues singers: Muddy Waters; Etta James; Bessie Smith; B.B. King; Ma Rainey.

FOLK

Be careful who you ask to define folk music. To an ethnomusicologist, someone who studies the traditional music of various ethnic groups, it may mean any traditional music, performed by any culture, anywhere on earth. But if you ask most Americans to define folk music, they'll probably come up with the "music of the common man" as performed by the likes of Pete Seeger, Woody Guthrie, and Joan Baez. Both are correct, but both miss the rich body of American folk music, which draws heavily on the country's immigrant history. American folk music has deep roots in Celtic, German, British, French, and other genres of folk music. A hundred years from now, that list will probably be longer and represent more of the globe.

Just so you know—most American folk musicians play guitar well enough to accompany themselves. How else are you going to do the stereotypical coffee-house gigs?

Folk folks: Woody Guthrie; Joan Baez; Bob Dylan.

CELTIC MUSIC

Celtic music is a form of folk music that grew up in the British Isles, the land of the Celts. Celtic music has always had an audience, but that audience has grown tremendously in recent years. The Celtic Colors International Festival on Cape Breton Island, Nova Scotia and Irish Fest in Milwaukee, Wisconsin are two of the world's largest festivals of Celtic music. Many cities have their own Celtic music festivals. This music is infectious, melodic, and largely sung in English. If you want to sing Celtic music, you need to start listening to the popular Celtic bands and singers to get a feel for the style. You'll notice that there are traditional and contemporary groups singing Celtic music. You can learn style, musicianship, and showmanship from both.

Celtic groups: Gaelic Storm; Cherish the Ladies; The Clancy Brothers.

GOSPEL

Gospel is the realm of roof-raising singers. The style, which grew out of the African-American churches during the early part of the 20th century, features a highly emotional vocal that's often backed up by a chorus. An element of improvisation plays into the style as well. Today, the term Gospel is sometimes used to describe contemporary Christian worship music, but to musicians, the soul-stirring, rousing music of Southern Christian churches is all that fills the bill. If you want to sing gospel, you had better start attending church. Each church has its own preferred singers and style and long-standing tradition of favorite songs and hymns.

In the world of "old-time" Gospel, no one beats Mahalia Jackson. James Cleveland, who died in 1991, was called the "King of Gospel" by fans.

R&B/SOUL

Gospel is closely linked to R&B (rhythm and blues) and soul music, both of which grew from the same musical roots as gospel. In fact, most definitions of R&B call it combination of jazz gospel and blues, and most definitions of soul call it a combination of R&B and gospel. It should be no surprise then that many R&B and blues singers got their start in gospel.

R&B/Soul singers: Bobby Womack; James Brown; Aretha Franklin; Marvin Gay; Otis Redding; Etta James.

BROADWAY (MUSICAL THEATER)

Musical Theater tunes range from sweet songs like "Till There Was You" from the musical *The Music Man*, to the hilarious, pseudo-German "Der Guten Tag Hop-Clop" from *The Producers*, and from the rock songs of *Rent* to the Elphaba's poignant numbers in *Wicked*. Anything that can be expressed onstage can be expressed in musical theater numbers. As a singer, it's your job to know what parts are right for ingénue (young, female leads), leading man (the tall handsome types), characters roles (wonderful scene-stealing parts), etc. Learn songs written for your voice (soprano, tenor, etc.) that are part of characters you might play. Then get out there and audition.

You can find recordings of show tunes by looking for individual shows or by looking for collections by specific singers or composers. Richard Rodgers and Oscar Hammerstein II; Stephen Sondheim; Andrew Lloyd Webber; John Kander and Fred Webb wrote some of the genre's classics.

Broadway singers of the past include: Yul Brenner; Jerry Orbach; Mary Martin; John Raitt; Ethel Merman. Contemporary Broadway singers include: Nathan Lane; Audra McDonald; Bernadette Peters; Bebe Neuwirth; Rebecca Luker; George Dvorsky.

JAZZ

The improvisatory stuff of smoky clubs, jazz has an aficionado following that's every bit as devoted as the folks that follow classical music. Jazz lovers can tell you when Charlie Parker recorded what and with whom. More than perhaps any other genre, jazz is unique unto the performer. Listen to ten jazz singers each give a performance of a single song and you will find ten different meanings to the song.

Singing jazz, although it sounds completely free, requires either a phenomenal ear for harmony and improvisation or a lot of careful study—or perhaps both. As with any genre, the way to start learning is to start listening. Find a few singers whose style appeals to you and begin listening to what they do and how they express themselves. Finding a jazz musician to study with, particularly to learn the nuanced styles that are part of jazz singers vocabulary, would be your best plan of attack in this genre.

Among the great jazz singers are: Billy Holiday; Ella Fitzgerald; Frank Sinatra; Sarah Vaughan; Johnny Hartman.

CLASSICAL

In the world of classical music, singers tend to specialize in early music (written in the Middle Ages, Renaissance or Baroque eras—or before about 1750), new music (classical music written since about 1975), opera, oratorio (pieces that tell a story like an opera but are performed on a concert stage without scenery or costumes), or song literature. Many libraries have extensive CD collections of classical music that are available for checkout. Even if singing opera or other forms of classical music isn't on your personal radar, it's not a bad idea to listen to some of these highly trained singers.

Early Music: Emma Kirkby; Boston Camerata; The King's Noyse; Anne Azema

Remember that recordings didn't appear until the early years of the 20th century. As a result, we have to make educated assumptions and decisions about how any music written and performed before that time might have sounded.

Classical singers who specialize in opera are the powerhouses of the vocal world. Singing without amplification, the most powerful of these singers can make their sound soar above the orchestra accompanying them. There's no shortage of opera and oratorio recordings on the market, but they tend to be packaged in pricey boxed sets. A good bet if you want to sample operas and oratorios is to go to your local library and check out several collections of "opera's greatest hits," or "great opera arias," or the entire opera or oratorio. DVDs are also available of many of the famous operas. Recordings from the Metropolitan Opera (New York City) are usually a good bet.

Great opera singers: Placido Domingo; Jessye Norman; Samuel Ramey; Joan Sutherland; Bryn Terfel.

Singers who specialize in song literature are masters of bringing tremendous meaning to short songs, some no more than a couple of minutes long. They have to be able to convey humor, pathos, despair, and any other human emotion a song might deal with. They include: Janet Baker; Barbara Bonney; Dietrich Fischer-Dieskau; Thomas Hampson; Peter Schreier; Dawn Upshaw.

Classical singers have to be able to sing in English, German, French, and Italian, because these are the languages in which most of the classical literature is written. If you want to sing some of the classical literature without mastering an entire language, you might learn the International Phonetic Alphabet (IPA) instead. The IPA assigns pronunciation symbols to various sounds and allows singers to pronounce a foreign language well, even if they don't speak it. You'll still have to translate the song or find a translation, though, so that you know what you're singing about.

CONTEMPORARY CHRISTIAN

Somewhere between gospel and pop lies contemporary Christian music. This is the stuff of church services and Christian rallies, accompanied by guitar, bass, and keyboards. Although the "Christian rock" genre has been gaining momentum in recent years, much of the contemporary Christian genre remains a soft-rock oriented sound. Many churches put together small combos to lead the singing at worship services, sometimes paying the performers to reduce turnover.

Artists include: Amy Grant; Michael W. Smith; Casting Crowns; Point of Grace.

WORLD MUSIC

Cultures around the world have developed types of singing, and with them distinct sounds, that until fairly recent years were rarely heard on concert stages. Now classified under the banner of "World Music," the genre has found a new audience in recent years. Styles from Reggae to Zydeco to Native American singing and drumming are finding a home on American concert stages.

For an interesting taste of world music try: Joanne Shenandoah (Native American); Ladysmith Black Mambazo (South African); Chubby Carrier and the Bayou Swamp Band (Zydeco).

Finding music that suits your voice begins with understanding what your voice does best. You may love alternative rock but have a voice best suited to country or jazz. Trying to shoehorn your voice into a style it can't do can damage it forever, creating a rough, uncontrollable sound. Listening to singers you enjoy in the genres you want to sing is a good way to get a handle on what the various styles require. Once you've narrowed the field and have listened to several of the great performers in whatever genre appeals to you, try out a song or two in that style. Learn them as best you can and then take them to someone who teaches or coaches that style of singing to help you determine if you're on the right path.

For advice on finding a voice teacher or coach, see **Chapter 9: Singing Smart**.

CHAPTER 6
WORKING ON YOUR SONGS

What's Ahead:
- Listen to this
- Slow down!
- Technically speaking
- Going beyond the notes and words
- It matters when you sing
- Hands and eyes
- Don't forget to memorize
- Did you hear that?

Songs are amazing things—entities, really. Each time someone new sings a song they bring their own life experience and abilities to it, making it something new and different than it was before—hopefully something worth listening to. The song "I Will" (written by Paul McCartney for his wife-to-be Linda Eastman and credited to Lennon and McCartney) is a great example of a song becoming something entirely different with each new rendition. McCartney's original interpretation was completely heartfelt. Alison Krauss gave a wistful take on the song, accompanied by banjo and steel guitar. Maureen McGovern brought a sense of nostalgia to the song, Tim Curry (of *Rocky Horror Picture Show* fame) gave the tune a Jamaican flavor, while South African singer Hugh Masakela turned it into something simple and plaintive. Ben Taylor, son of singer/songwriter James Taylor sounded hopeful and slightly naïve on the 1995 soundtrack of the film *Bye Bye, Love*. More than a decade later, Diana Ross delivered the song in a satiny, intimate style on her 2007 recording *I Love You*. The song isn't unique in its track record of being *covered* (in the music industry, a new recording of a song that's already been recorded is called a "cover") by another artist. In fact, there are countless covers of countless songs, because every new version brings something new to the music. For a delightful taste of how different interpretations can affect the impact of a song, listen to the album *A Song for My Father* (produced for Target stores), in which the children of famous artists like Jim Croce, Bob Marley, Leonard Cohen, Arlo Guthrie, and others take turns at songs made famous by their parents.

Take your time learning your music. Listen to several different recordings of it, if you can, with the music in front of you. If there is only one version available, which is the case with lots of rock and pop tunes, then you need to be a little careful about listening to the recording. Listening to several different performers take their turns at a song can open your ears to new possibilities as you interpret the song for yourself. But if you listen to one recording over and over again, chances are you'll begin to sing it just as the original performer did. Imitation may be the sincerest form of flattery in some areas of life, but in music it just makes for bland copies. If you step onstage singing a song just like Barbra Streisand, Josh Groban, or perhaps Luther Vandross sang it, all your audience will be able to do is compare you to the original. You won't win.

LISTEN TO THIS

If there is only one version of the song out there, skip the listening-to-recordings phase of learning and go straight to listening to the accompaniment and listening to recordings of yourself. In the musical *The Music Man*, the leading man promotes a method of teaching called the "Think System," in which the kids of River City learn to play their band instruments without making a single sound. They simply think about what they will sound like when they play. This is, of course, part of a plan to hoodwink the townspeople into paying for lessons and instruments that the children will never be taught to play. But in real life, there's actually a lot of merit to the "Think System" of practice. Singers can learn lyrics, rhythms, melodies, and how the melody fits with the accompaniment just by listening.

Singers can also make decisions on their own interpretations of a song through the listening process. Ask your accompanist or band to record the accompaniment for you. Study the words and music without making a sound, to make sure you understand the piece and what thoughts and emotions it's trying to convey. Silent study with the music in front of you and the recording of the accompaniment playing is a great opportunity to develop your own thoughts on how you want to sing the song. Once you start singing the song with your band or accompanist, you'll be pretty occupied by singing in tune, keeping time with the accompaniment, coming in correctly on each entrance, etc. Your best chance to create a song interpretation that's all yours is when you're listening to the accompaniment and looking at the music.

SLOW DOWN!

Take your time learning new songs. Live with the song and what it's saying for a few weeks before you commit to an interpretation. Spend a little time in that delightful stage of learning a song when you're humming it in the car and mumbling the lyrics as you take a walk. The quicker you learn a song, the quicker you'll forget it. Learning a new song is like making a great cup of tea—you have to let it steep a while to get the full flavor out of the brew.

TECHNICALLY SPEAKING

Lots of the songs you sing will be mostly easy with one or two hard spots tucked in. You're audience doesn't need to know which sections of a song are hardest for you to sing, so make a habit of pulling out those sections and working on them separately from the rest of the song. The easy parts simply don't need as much as practice as the hard parts. Put parentheses around the tough spots in your songs (using a pencil, of course) and spend some time in each practice session working on just those marked parts. It's okay to go for several days without singing a song straight through, if you're working on the details—in fact, it's recommended!

Recording yourself in practice sessions, performances, voice lessons, and coachings can be a great tool. When you're singing, your ears will pick up sound waves from the air around you, but also from the vibrations traveling through the bones of your head and jaw. The mix of those two sets of sound waves can be really deceptive. The other thing you'll notice when you hear yourself on a recording is that the big musical moment that felt like such a great expression of emotion will probably sound pretty tame in a replay. Most of us don't make grand, emotional statements on a regular basis in our daily lives. When we're called upon to do that while singing, we're a little uncomfortable letting loose and really going for it. Remember, you're singing to the people in the back of the room as well as those in the front—make sure they all know what you think about the song you're singing.

A great way to find out how you really sound on any given song is to record it and then *don't* listen to the recording for a day or two. Patience is a virtue, especially when learning songs. If you listen right away, your mind will either hear what you thought you were doing rather than what you were doing, or it will hear only the flaws that you were aware of as you sang and not the things you did well. Give it some time and then listen critically, thinking about both what you like about the recording and what you want to do better. There will be some of both.

Use the best device you can, a cassette recorder, mini disc, or digital recorder that distorts sound as little as possible. Even the best singers in the world can sound embarrassingly bad in a poor recording. It can be helpful to record your warm-ups from time to time too, as a means of listening critically to your strengths and weaknesses. In addition to having your band or pianist record the accompaniments to the songs you're singing, you can also have your accompanist record the piano part to warm-ups for you. There are lots of books of vocal warm-ups and exercises on the market, most of which have simple piano accompaniments included. Changing the content of warm-ups from time to time helps the process to stay fresh and allows you work on different elements of singing as you need to.

Your accompanist is a trained professional and should be paid for the service of providing recordings. Always ask what a pianist charges before you make the recordings to avoid any disputes afterward.

GOING BEYOND THE NOTES AND WORDS

Musical elements of a song, like the dynamics or expressive details you want to bring to it, are worked on when you're singing straight through the song. Figure out what you want to say with the song, which lyrics you think are most important, and which phrases you think have the most meaning. Then draw your listeners' attention to them. Remember, you don't have to sing loudly to get attention. Singers like Cleo Lane have mastered the art of drawing listeners into their own thoughts and emotions through subtle, meaningful details in their performances.

IT MATTERS WHEN YOU SING

It's not a good idea to leave your practicing for late in the evening. By the very end of the day you're tired, so you won't be concentrating nor will you be standing, breathing, and singing your best. It's also not a good idea to roll out of bed in the morning and jump right into practicing. Make sure you allow a little time for your body to wake up before singing—perhaps a brisk walk to get the blood flowing and some breakfast to make sure you're fueled up. Always make sure you're well-hydrated, which can be accomplished by drinking plenty of water, tea, or other beverages that won't coat your throat with gooey dairy residue or a sticky, sugary coating.

Once you have learned a piece and are polishing it for a performance, practice going straight through it from front to finish. Don't stop if you make a mistake or if something doesn't go quite the way you wanted it to. You have to get used to moving on, no matter what. You won't be able to stop in the performance, so get used to finishing the song.

HANDS AND EYES

As you get close to your performance, it's a good idea to begin thinking about where you want to aim your eyes as you sing. Some singers find that making eye contact with audience members is really helpful in giving a meaningful rendition of a song. It makes them feel as though they're talking directly to those people. But other singers find that looking into the eyes of audience members is uncomfortable. They prefer to keep their eyes just above the heads of the audience. Giving a run-through performance can help you determine which approach is most comfortable for you.

You might think that hands have nothing to do with singing a good performance, but you'd be wrong. If you find yourself in the position of singing without a microphone or guitar in your hands, as is the case in many auditions, church gigs, recitals, and other situations, you have to decide what to do with your hands. They can't just hang at your sides like the catch of the day, nor can they be in constant, fluttering, nervous motion. So what should you do with them? Try a little subtle choreography to suit the music you're performing.

Just as it's important to practice your songs with the breathing in place, it's important to practice your songs with the gestures and hand positions you intend to use onstage. Rehearsing your hand positions may sound like a silly detail to fuss over, but it will make you much more poised and comfortable onstage, giving you one less thing to distract or worry you.

DON'T FORGET TO MEMORIZE

Singers memorize. Unless you're singing in a church balcony, recording studio, or some other spot where you can't be seen by your audience, you will need to memorize your music. In auditions too, memorizing music makes you look prepared, confident, and professional—all the qualities that will make you hire-able. The music will become a barrier between you and your audience at worst, a distraction at best.

For singers, memorization involves two elements: the tune and the lyrics. You will probably find that of the two, the lyrics are the bigger challenge. There are several ways to simplify the process of memorizing lyrics—and no, you can't just write them on your palm, or lay them at your feet and sneak glances.

The first step is to make a road map of the song. Does it have verses and a chorus? Is there a bridge in the song that prepares the listener for the return of the main tune? Look over the song and write down a roadmap of the music. Understanding the map will help you cement the song in your memory. In a ballad, or any song that tells a story, knowing the progression of the story helps a lot in memorizing the lyrics.

You have to know what you're singing about in order to give meaning to the lyrics. Whether you're singing in English, Latin, Italian, Hebrew, or some other language, you have to know what the words of the song mean in order to give a cogent performance and certainly in order to memorize them. Many pieces with lyrics in foreign languages will have English translations in the music. Some translations can be found online, others will require a little time with a dictionary. Whatever the case, translate the lyrics into English so that you know, word for word, what you're singing.

Working on the lyrics away from the music can help as well. Walking and chanting the lyrics, mentally of course, can be a helpful aid. As you walk, your footsteps will fall in an even rhythm that you can use as the beat under the lyrics. Chanting the lyrics out loud, also in rhythm, can also help you memorize them.

DID YOU HEAR THAT?

Don't forget to listen, not just to yourself, but to other singers as well. It's easy to figure out that if you want to sing jazz, you should listen to jazz and if you want to sing country, you should listen to country. But don't limit yourself. Before you are a jazz, country, classical, rock or folk musician, you are a singer. Listen to singers. You can learn a lot about nuance, style, vocal technique, communication, and showmanship from anyone who sings. One of the most important things to listen for is smooth, effortless singing that takes the listener deep inside the music. Remember, you can learn from great performers or poor ones. Hearing something that sounds absolutely dreadful can sometimes be a powerful, not to mention memorable, example of what doesn't work.

Carry a little notebook and take notes when listening to singers. Over time, this will become your own personal stylebook.

The following song, "Minstrel Boy," is an Irish ballad. The heartbreaking tune and melody have been used in everything from concert performances to television (*Star Trek: The Next Generation*) and film (*Black Hawk Down*). The song's lyrics were written by Thomas Moore, reputedly in remembrance of friends killed in the Irish Rebellion of 1798. The third verse was added during the Civil War, by Irishmen fighting in the American Civil War. The tune is actually an earlier Irish song, "The Moreen."

There are several performances of this song worth listening to, including John McDermott and Celtic songwriter Charlie Zahm and folk musician Danny Quinn. Notice the differences between the various interpretations as you listen.

Listen to Track 20 on the CD that accompanies this book. You may want to sing along with the singer a time or two before moving to the following track, which provides just the accompaniment to the song. As you work with the accompaniment track, work on bringing your own thoughts on the music to your performance.

Minstrel Boy

Traditional

Copyright © 2003 by HAL LEONARD CORPORATION
International Copyright Secured All Rights Reserved

You can also polish your practicing skills with Sting's lyrical 1993 hit "Fields of Gold." Before you work on this with an accompanist, listen to Sting's recording of the piece as well as singer Eva Cassidy's performance.

Fields of Gold

Music and Lyrics by
STING

You'll re - mem - ber me, when the west wind moves __ up -
stay with me, will you be my love __ a -

on the fields __ of bar - ley. You'll for - get the sun in his
mong the fields __ of bar - ley? We'll for - get the sun in his

© 1993 STEERPIKE LTD.
Administered by EMI MUSIC PUBLISHING LIMITED
All Rights Reserved   International Copyright Secured   Used by Permission

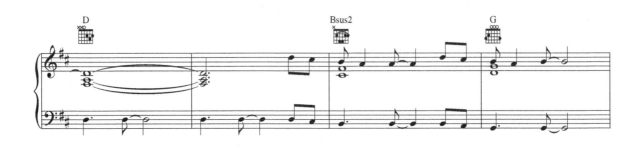

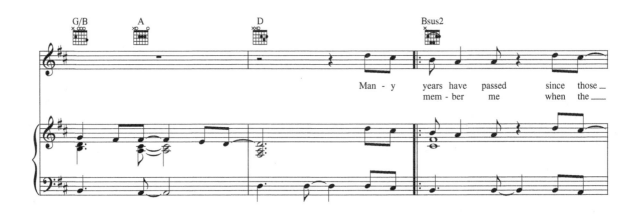

Man - y years have passed since those ___
mem - ber me when the ___

___ sum - mer days a - mong the fields ___ of bar - ley. See the
___ west wind moves up - on the fields ___ of bar - ley. You can

Expanding Your Skills

CHAPTER 7
MAKING MUSIC

What's Ahead:
- Shaping a phrase
- Making music your own

Have you ever noticed that some performers can absolutely break your heart with a single song? Yet, someone else singing that same song may be only mildly interesting. The reason for the seeming sleight of hand is that producing notes and making music are *not* the same thing. In fact, for some they're not related in the least. Reading notes and producing the sounds they indicate is the craft of music making. Taking those notes and creating an interesting performance that's sensitive and meaningful is an art. A chapter on making music is not going to make a great artist out of you or anyone else, but it may open your ears to the art of music making, which is the first step.

> *Dynamics* and *phrasing* are two closely related key elements in music making. Dynamics is the aspect of musical expression resulting from variation in the volume of sound. Phrasing is the art of taking a musical line, essentially a string of notes, and giving it shape and direction.

Listen to the singer on Track 22 perform "Shenandoah" with no thought to phrasing whatsoever. This is something you'll want to avoid. Shaping a phrase is a combination of dynamic *accents* (musical stresses) and a bit of *rubato* (holding onto a note slightly longer than the music calls for, in order to create musical effect).

SHAPING A PHRASE

Say the flowing sentence aloud with a strong emphasis on a different word each time: I don't have any idea who you're talking about. (*I* don't have any idea who you're talking about. I *don't* have any idea who you're talking about... etc.) Each time you put the accent on a different word, you change the shape of the phrase. Just as an actor might try out the accent on each possible word to see what effect best suits the meaning of the sentence, a singer might try out the accent on each word, and its corresponding note, in a phrase of music.

Once you've decided which word in the phrase is most important, you can experiment a little further by making a *crescendo* (a gradual increase in volume) leading up to that note, and a *diminuendo* (a gradual decrease in volume) on the notes moving away from the accented note. You can also make the accent sudden, with no crescendo leading up to it, or shape that phrase any way that suits your taste.

Many singers mark phrasings in their music with long, arced lines penciled in above the music to indicate where a single phrase begins and ends. Crescendos (a gradual increase in volume) and diminuendos (a gradual decrease in volume) are marked below the music with a symbol that looks like a long V, laid on its side. The wide end of the V indicates more volume, the closed point indicates less volume.

The many levels of volume between very soft and very loud are indicated with abbreviations for the Italian word for soft. Piano, which means "soft," is written with a single *p*. Forte, which means loud, is written with a single *f*. To help sort out how loud and soft to make the music, the abbreviations may be double or tripled or paired with the letter m for the Italian word *mezzo* (middle or medium).

ppp – very, very soft	*mf* – moderately loud
pp – very soft	*f* – loud
p – soft	*ff* – very loud
mp – moderately soft	*fff* – very, very loud

Accents, which indicate a stress on a single note, are indicated with a small sideways V above or below the note. The accent mark looks like a miniature diminuendo mark, which is exactly what it is. The accent mark tells you to make the beginning of the note (known as the *attack*) louder than what came before it and louder than what comes after it.

Music making involves more than just getting louder and softer. It also includes subtle changes in the tempo and rhythm of a piece to help focus the listener on notes or lyrics that are important.

A slight hold on a single note may be indicated with a *tenuto* mark:

A longer hold on a note may be indicated with a *fermata*:

A gradual slowing or slackening of tempo may be indicated with a *rubato* mark:

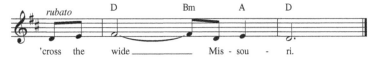

When you see the words *a tempo* after a section of music in which the tempo has been changed, it indicates that the music should return to the original tempo.

Listen to Tracks 23 and 24, watching the music for "Shenandoah" in the following examples. Notice how the singer interprets the various markings to change the shape of the phrase.

Shenandoah

Copyright © 2000 by HAL LEONARD CORPORATION
International Copyright Secured   All Rights Reserved

American Folksong

Now sing along to the accompaniment to "Shenandoah" in Track 25, using the interpretive markings found in the example printed above. Experiment with your own interpretation too, marking it in pencil on the music on page 59.

Shenandoah

Copyright © 2000 by HAL LEONARD CORPORATION
International Copyright Secured   All Rights Reserved

American Folksong

Oh, Shen - an - doah, ___ I long to hear you, ___ a - way ___ you roll - ing riv - er. Oh, Shen - an - doah, ___ I long to hear you. ___ A - way, ___ I'm bound a - way, 'cross the wide ___ Mis - sou - ri.

Always use a pencil to mark your music. You may change your mind about markings over time, or may have to sing from borrowed or rented music. In either case, being able to erase your markings is very important.

The following song, "What a Wonderful World" (not to be confused with another great song, "Wonderful World"), is a standard from the many fabulous tunes that are now known as the Great American Songbook. There are quite a few wonderful recordings of this song that you can listen to as you study the music, including ones by Louis Armstrong, Eva Cassidy, Tony Bennett, LeAnn Rimes, Willie Nelson, Rod Stewart, and even Jerry Garcia. The number of recordings of this songs that are available make it a great song to study as you learn to create your own interpretation. Listen. Decide which renditions speak to you and why. Take notes. Mark the music in pencil as you begin to work with an accompanist. Your ideas about the song will probably change as you work on it, which is a perfectly natural part of the learning process. You'll be very glad all those marks are written **in pencil**. Be sure to take a little time away from the song. Make those marks in your part and then put the song aside for a few days. When you come back to it and sing it with your accompanist again, your markings will remind you of the decisions you made. You may choose to keep those markings and that interpretation, or to alter some of them or start over. You may also sing a song the same way many times (possibly for years) and then, one day, decide to rethink it.

What a Wonderful World

Words and Music by GEORGE DAVID WEISS
and BOB THIELE

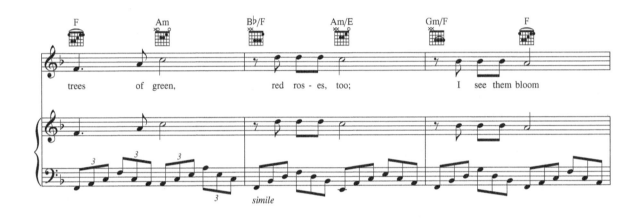

Copyright © 1967 by Range Road Music Inc., Bug Music-Quartet Music and Abilene Music, Inc.
Copyright Renewed
International Copyright Secured   All Rights Reserved
Used by Permission

It's important to run through songs with accompanist or band members, so that you all know what to expect from one another when you're performing. If they know how you're approaching a song, they can support your phrasing with their own music making. This becomes a very important issue when you're singing with a pianist or organist in a situation like a wedding. The person accompanying you needs to know how you want to interpret each song in order to support your performance. Penciling your own phrasings and dynamics into the accompanist's part before you meet to rehearse is a good, time-saving idea.

MAKING MUSIC YOUR OWN

"I'll Get By (As Long as I Have You)" was published in 1928. Songwriters Fred Ahlert (music) and Roy Turk (lyrics) gave us such other classics as "Walkin' My Baby Back Home" and "I Don't Know Why (I Just Do)." The song has had a long, interesting life in recordings. Listen to the early Ruth Etting recording, as well as later ones by Peggy Lee, Connie Francis, and Keely Smith. In 1944, a re-release of Harry James's 1940 recording of the song (Dick Haymes on vocals) went to #1 on the charts. A 1943 recording by Bill Kenny and the Ink Spots is well worth hearing, as is the one about a decade later by the Platters. Listening to these different interpretations of the song will help you make your own decisions as you fashion an expressive interpretation.

I'll Get By

(As Long as I Have You)

Lyric by ROY TURK
Music by FRED E. AHLERT

TRO - © Copyright 1928 (Renewed) Cromwell Music, Inc., New York, NY, Pencil Mark Music, Inc., Bronxville, NY, Azure Pearl Music, Beeping Good Music and David Ahlert Music
All Rights for Azure Pearl Music, Beeping Good Music and David Ahlert Music Administered by Bluewater Music Services Corp.
International Copyright Secured
All Rights Reserved Including Public Performance For Profit
Used by Permission

Making music with a song means understanding its genre and the style that genre requires. That said, "Your Cheatin' Heart" is a country music classic, written in 1952 by Hank Williams Sr. Listen to recordings by such country, or country-influenced, musicians as Hank Williams Sr. (and Jr.), as well as Patsy Cline, Elvis Presley, and Jerry Lee Lewis. Then listen to Ray Charles perform the piece. Acknowledging the roots of a song doesn't mean mimicking a musical stereotype. Listen to as many recordings of the piece you can, following along in the music, and make your own decision about how to sing this classic tune.

Your Cheatin' Heart

Words and Music by
HANK WILLIAMS

Copyright © 1952 Sony/ATV Music Publishing LLC and Hiriam Music in the U.S.A.
Copyright Renewed
All Rights on behalf of Hiriam Music Administered by Rightsong Music Inc.
All Rights outside the U.S.A. Administered by Sony/ATV Music Publishing LLC
All Rights on behalf of Sony/ATV Music Publishing LLC Administered by Sony/ATV Music Publishing LLC,
8 Music Square West, Nashville, TN 37203
International Copyright Secured   All Rights Reserved

Refining Your Sound and Style

CHAPTER 8
DICTION

What's Ahead:
- A second set of ears
- Tongue twisters
- Vowels
- Be flexible

Have you ever wondered why the Beatles sounded so British when they spoke, but so American when they sang? Diction. They sang with pronunciations that are known as "Casual American." Pronunciation—technically, "diction"—is also the reason that a country singer from the Bronx sounds like a country singer from Nashville when he or she sings and someone singing opera sounds like a native of whatever language they happen to be singing in at a given moment.

Diction has another function too. We've all heard people massacre the lyrics of a rock song, singing, "The hardest rock and roll is in Cleveland," to the Huey Lewis tune "The Heart of Rock and Roll Is Still Beating," for instance. Diction lets your audience hear the words in addition to the melody you're singing, allowing you to communicate with both.

Diction is also part of what allows Broadway singers to make every word heard in the back of a theater, or someone singing a solo in a large cathedral able to make their lyrics intelligible. Singers must always balance the style of music they're singing with the performance space and adjust the crispness of their pronunciations to make themselves understood.

The live acoustic of a cathedral requires extra separation between phrases, and sometimes between words, to allow the reverberation (echo) of one phrase to fade away a bit before the singer starts the next one. Theater singers work hard to enunciate lyrics, because they provide necessary insights into the characters and plot. They end up with performances that are perfect for the genre, but would sound ridiculously over-enunciated in other situations. Opera singers often alter vowels slightly in order to create the biggest, most ringing sound possible. In these days of *supertitles* (electronically generated translations that are shown above the stage, or perhaps on the backs of seats in the opera house), opera singers are focusing on their sound, bringing meaning to their arias through musical nuance rather than through crystal-clear lyrics.

A SECOND SET OF EARS
Many singers will ask a person they trust to listen as they rehearse with their band or accompanist, to see what it sounds like to someone in the audience. The more acoustically alive, or resonant, a room is, the more singers have to separate words and use crisp consonants. Finding a large, empty room, like a church or a gymnasium, and trying to speak or sing to someone on the far side of the room can help a singer strike a good balance between too much consonant use and too little.

TONGUE TWISTERS

Consonants also become an issue when singing long strings of complicated lyrics. Singers have to be able to get words out of their mouths without adding tension to their vocal production. A helpful way of working on diction is to do the same thing actors, broadcasters, and other public speakers do: warm up using "tongue twisters," phrases that really challenge the tongue and mouth. The trick to working on tongue twisters is to begin slowly and crisply, gradually picking up speed as the phrases become comfortable to say. Work on one of these per day as part of your warm-up.

> Tongue twisters are great time-fillers while stuck in traffic.
> One gem of a tongue twister is "Peter Piper:"
>
> Peter Piper picked a peck of pickled peppers.
> A peck of pickled peppers, Peter Piper picked.
> If Peter Piper picked a peck of pickled peppers,
> Where's the peck of pickled peppers Peter Piper picked?

Each of the following phrases is a tongue twister. Repeat each several times, slowly, without pausing. Really move your lips and tongue to get the clearest enunciation possible. As they become comfortable when done slowly, begin to pick up the pace. Always speed up gradually, taking it just a little faster and mastering the phrase at the new speed before trying to speed it up any more.

Blue Buick, Black Buick.
I saw Susie sitting in a shoe-shine shop. Where she sits she shines, and where she shines she sits.
Seth at Sainsbury's sells thick socks.
Real race winners rarely want red wine right away!
Tie twine to three tree twigs.
Five frantic frogs fled from fifty fierce fishes.
Eleven benevolent elephants.
Weary real rear wheel.
Double bubble. Triple trouble.
Three free fleas flew through three tree's leaves.
Three Plymouth sleuths thwart Luther's slithering.
Thin grippy thick slippery.
Fresh French flies fried fritters.
Toy boat. Toy boat.
Gig whip. Gig whip.
Black background. Brown background.
Six slimy snails sailed silently.

VOWELS

Consonants are only part of the diction equation. When we sing, we sustain vowel sounds. Therefore, our vowels require constant attention.

Fortunately for singers, it's easier to navigate diphthongs and triphthongs in lyrics than it is to pronounce those two words. A diphthong (pronounced DIFF-thong) is a vowel that's actually a combination of two vowel sounds in a single syllable. Try saying the words "toy" or "now" slowly and you notice that the vowels needs to change shape in mid-word.

A triphthong (pronounced TRIFF-thong) is a series of three vowel sounds that are joined together in a single syllable. The words "higher" "our" are examples of triphthongs. The difficulty of singing diphthongs and triphthongs is that they have to be executed smoothly and naturally, and often differently than they are in daily speech.

Common diphthongs include words like: my, tie, by, sigh, and why. Common triphthongs include words like: fire, tire, tower, and hour. Some accents, particularly American country and western accents, turn these into one-syllable words (my = mah; fire = fahr, etc.). Those one-syllable pronunciations may be handy when singing country songs, but if you're crooning a jazz standard like "Night and Day," or belting out "Send in the Clowns," you're going to have to learn to handle diphthongs and triphthongs gracefully and naturally.

I fight fire.

Pick a note that's comfortable for you to sustain. Using just that one note, sing the words "I fight fire," holding each word for several beats. Notice that in each word your mouth and tongue begin to form a second vowel sound, "ee." On the word "fire," your tongue will move to form a third vowel before the "r" as well. Listen to the singer on the CD sing the same phrase. Notice how the singer handles the diphthongs and triphthong. In each case, "ah" is the most prominent vowel sound. The others take a backseat—they come late in the word and are not emphasized.

Sighing. Crying. Dying.

Listen to the singer on Track 30 sing "Russian Lullaby." Notice that the word "lullaby" in this American version of a Russian folksong ends in a diphthong, each of which is sustained. Make them smooth and natural. Go to the "ee" sound near the end of the note, sustaining the "ah" sound of the first half of the diphthong.

Russian Lullaby

Copyright © 2000 by HAL LEONARD CORPORATION
International Copyright Secured   All Rights Reserved

American version of a Russian Folksong

Take a look at "Somewhere Out There," by James Horner, Barry Mann, and Cynthia Weil. It was heard in the 1986 animated film *An American Tail*. Listen to the version of the song from the film, where it was sung by a little animated mouse. Listen to the recording by James Ingram and Linda Ronstadt. Cute as the film version is, you will obviously be shooting for something a bit more polished—something more along the lines of the Ronstadt/Ingram version. The song can be sung by a single performer or performed as duet.

Somewhere Out There

from AN AMERICAN TAIL

Music by BARRY MANN and JAMES HORNER
Lyric by CYNTHIA WEIL

Copyright © 1986 USI A MUSIC PUBLISHING and USI B MUSIC PUBLISHING
All Rights Controlled and Administered by UNIVERSAL MUSIC CORP. and SONGS OF UNIVERSAL, INC.
All Rights Reserved   Used by Permission

BE FLEXIBLE

Adjusting pronunciation to the genre of the song you're singing is a big factor in making your performance credible. Hearing "Maria" from the musical *West Side Story* sung with a country twang, or Clapton's "Layla" sung with the precise diction of an opera singer is the stuff of television sitcoms. The way around such comical mistakes begins with your ears—listen to others singing the style of music you're working on.

"Walkin' After Midnight" was Patsy Cline's first major hit. As you search for other recordings, you may notice that very few other professional singers have recorded the song. This song was so strongly associated with Cline that many singers have steered away from recording it. Some notable versions are Bryan Adams' upbeat take on it and Madelaine Peyroux's slightly more jazzy rendition. No matter what direction you decide to take the song, you have to sell the dropped Gs on words like "walkin'," and make them sound like a natural part of speech, instead of an affectation put on for the song.

Walkin' After Midnight

Lyrics by DON HECHT
Music by ALAN W. BLOCK

I'll go out walk-in' _____ af - ter mid-night _____ in the
walk-in' _____ af - ter mid-night _____ in the

moon - light _____ just like we used to do. I'm al - ways
star - light _____ and pray that you may be some - where just

Copyright © 1956 Sony/ATV Music Publishing LLC
Copyright Renewed
All Rights Administered by Sony/ATV Music Publishing LLC, 8 Music Square West, Nashville, TN 37203
International Copyright Secured All Rights Reserved

Singers are often required to sing in languages other than one they grew up speaking. There are several approaches to this issue. One is learning the previously mentioned International Phonetic Alphabet (IPA), a series of symbols that will help guide a singer through just about any language they're faced with. The alphabet requires study, however. Singers need to continue working with it to keep it fresh in their minds. It's a bit like learning a foreign language in school—the moment you stop making regular use of it is the moment you start forgetting it.

The best option for learning foreign-language lyrics is to tape your teacher or coach speaking the lyrics. You may also be able to find a native speaker of the language to do the same thing for you.

If you have to rely on a recording of the song to learn the foreign-language lyric, be very careful not to model that performance when you start singing the song yourself. That performer's interpretation will become as embedded in your mind as the lyrics.

Once you have a recording of someone speaking the song's lyrics for you, you can write your own set of phonetic cues to help you get through the song. For instance, the phrase "'O sole mio" might be written "oh sew-lay mee-oh."

Cue up Track 32 and listen to the singer speaking the lyrics to this lovely Italian song. Write in your own phonetic cues. You will need to listen to it, write down a few things, listen again, and so on. Put it aside and listen to the track again in a day or two, looking at what you wrote. Fix anything that doesn't really reflect the correct pronunciation.

A performance is on Track 33. You can try it as a full-blown solo using the piano accompaniment on Track 34.

'O sole mio

Words by GIOVANNI CAPURRO
Music by EDUARDO DI CAPUA

Che bel - la co - sa 'na iur - na - ta 'e
While you are sleep - ing love's watch I am

so - le,____ N'a - ria se - re - na dop - po 'na tem -
keep - ing.____ Bright stars are peep - ing____ down from a -

Copyright © 2000 by HAL LEONARD CORPORATION
International Copyright Secured   All Rights Reserved

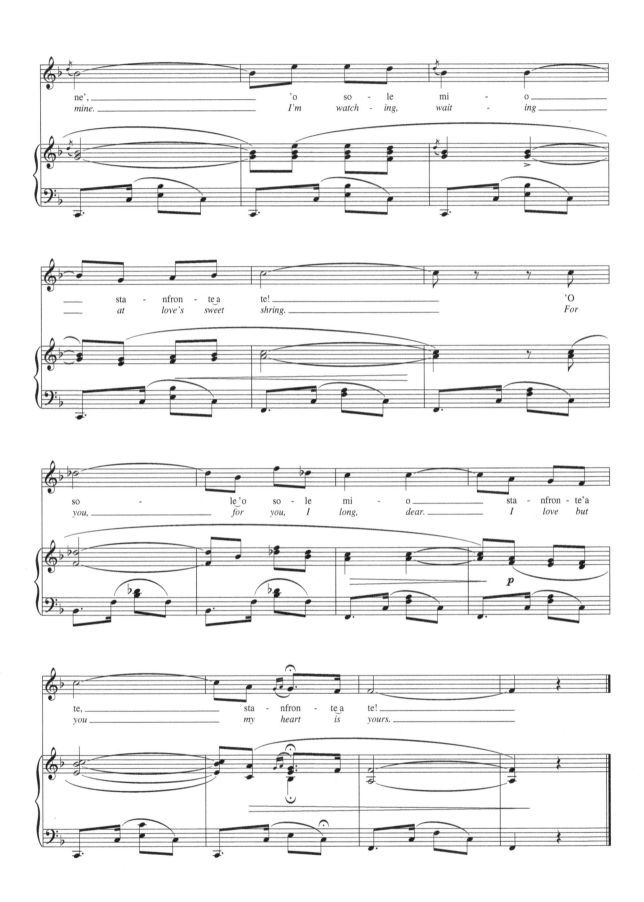

CHAPTER 9
SINGING SMART

What's Ahead:
- Finding a teacher
- Who's auditioning whom?
- What to expect from a teacher
- What to expect from a coach
- Vocal health

FINDING A TEACHER

As you get more serious about singing, you're going to come up with questions about the process and about what you, specifically, are doing that can't be answered in the pages of a book. You're going to need a teacher and possibly a coach to help you refine your sound and style. The difference between a teacher and a vocal coach is one of practicality. A teacher will help you develop good vocal technique and will teach you repertoire, or songs, designed to help you shape and polish your voice. Your relationship with your teacher will probably be a long one, meeting every week or two for several years. A vocal coach, on the other hand, is someone who can help you prepare for an audition or a performance and can tell you what's not working from a performing standpoint. A coach will polish specific pieces or get you ready for specific situations, but probably will not guide you through the long process of developing a solid vocal technique. You can go to a vocal coach a couple of times before an audition and not return for months. Many professional singers use both teachers and coaches throughout their careers, getting different things from both of them. As you're starting out, you should find a teacher that has a good reputation of turning out solid singers.

WHO'S AUDITIONING WHOM?

Finding the right teacher or coach is an important part of getting the most from your lessons. You need to look for someone who has worked in the genre you are interested in singing. Don't go an opera singer if you hope to sing country music, and don't go to a jazz singer if you are shooting for opera. Lessons can be expensive, starting at about $20 for a half-hour session and ranging to $200 or higher, so do your homework before you spend money.

You don't have to study with someone who sings the same voice part you do to get a lot out of the lessons. You need to find someone with solid training who has turned out some successful singers in recent years. A good way to start looking for a teacher is to talk to people who are doing the sort of singing you would like to be doing. Ask these singers who they have studied with, or coached with. You may find that they are teaching and coaching themselves. Talk to other singers to find out who they recommend, or maybe more importantly, recommend you stay away from. Just because someone can sing, it doesn't necessarily follow that they can teach. The opposite is also true. Some of the best teachers are often not great performers.

It is perfectly acceptable to ask for references (which, in the case of a voice teacher, would be current or former students) and a résumé. Don't be afraid to call some of these references. Ask them about the teaching style of the person you are considering trying out and about their studio habits. If you are paying for lessons and showing up on time for them, you want to know that your teacher is going to be there and be on time too. There will almost undoubtedly be times when a teacher has to cancel a lesson for a gig or for personal reasons, but those occasions should be the exception, not the rule. If someone's students tell you stories of showing up and finding no one there to teach the lessons, or stories of the teacher continually showing up late or being distracted during the lessons, keep looking. You need to find someone who is going to be punctual and dedicated to what they're doing.

It's also perfectly appropriate to ask a prospective teacher for a résumé. This a good way to find out if they have experience in the genre you're interested in and if they have done much professional work themselves. There's an old saying: "Those who cannot do, teach." It can be either true or untrue in the music world. Some of the best musicians around are terrible teachers and some are wonderful. Even the best of teachers won't work out for you if the two of you can't get along in the very personal setting of a voice lesson.

Once you have selected a teacher that you think might be good for you, ask if you can take a few sample lessons without making a six-month or longer commitment. Going back for several lessons will give you a chance to get comfortable with the teacher's style and personality and will give you a chance to get comfortable singing for them. If you're not comfortable after a few lessons, try a different teacher.

WHAT TO EXPECT FROM A TEACHER

A voice teacher will start by listening to your voice. The teacher will probably not give you a lot of actual songs to work on in the first few weeks of lessons. Instead, he or she will most likely give you exercises and warm-ups that you will do every day. Your teacher will most likely start each lesson with a few warm-ups and exercises as well. You will get used to the fact that teachers love to talk to students as they sing, reminding you to support, or relax, or pointing out some detail or another. KEEP SINGING! This is all quite normal behavior in a voice lesson or coaching. You'll get used to singing and adjusting what you're doing as your teacher calls out instructions. After getting to know your voice a bit, your teacher will start identifying the vocal issues you should be working on and will help you choose music that suits your voice. Just because you want to sing jazz standards doesn't mean every jazz standard is going to be good for your voice. Ella Fitzgerald and Judy Garland both sang jazz standards—but quite differently.

A voice teacher will also help you set up a warm-up routine that will keep your voice healthy, polish your strengths and work on your weaknesses. Your teacher will probably work a lot on your warm-up routine in your first few lessons, to help you build a good, solid foundation.

Any criticism you receive from a voice teacher is meant to make you sing better. If your teacher gives you nothing but praise, you're not going to learn anything. If you didn't have a voice worth working on, your teacher wouldn't be taking the time to make constructive criticism.

WHAT TO EXPECT FROM A COACH

You should audition a vocal coach in the same way you auditioned your teacher, looking for a good personality fit and someone with solid credentials. You can go to more than one coach. Remember that a coach who is adept at preparing people for jingle recordings may not be the best person to coach a music theater audition or role. No matter what coach you choose, they will expect you to walk in with your music pretty well prepared. They are there to help you polish it up—to create the final product. A vocal coach is also likely to have a good idea of what's going on in the vocal world in your area and can probably predict what various people who are hiring singers are looking for. Your vocal coach may give you tips on presentation and showmanship and may suggest clothing choices, hairstyle changes, or other image-related changes that may help you present yourself better. Like a voice teacher's criticisms, anything the coach points out is meant as constructive criticism. Don't be discouraged by the criticism—just use it to focus your practice and rehearsal sessions.

VOCAL HEALTH

Life would be a lot easier for singers if they could leave their voices at home once in a while. Taking care of your voice is not just something you think about when you're singing—it's a way of life. Unlike a guitarist or trumpeter, you can't tuck your instrument safely in a case, put it on a shelf and then go out for the evening. Your voice is with you at all times. Everything you eat, drink, and inhale or say has an impact on your vocal cords. Following a few basic rules, most of which are nothing more than basic common sense, can make a big difference in keeping your voice in good shape for your next gig and preserving it for years of singing.

THE SINGERS' CHECKLIST

DO:

- Get plenty of sleep.

- Stay hydrated. Drink plenty of water and warm liquids (herbal teas with no milk or cream). If you live in a very dry climate, a humidifier will help keep your vocal cords and sinuses from drying out at home.

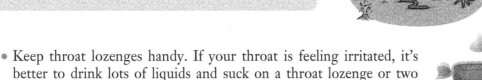
Even humid climates can become very dry indoors once winter hits and furnaces come on.

- Keep throat lozenges handy. If your throat is feeling irritated, it's better to drink lots of liquids and suck on a throat lozenge or two than to clear your throat and make it more irritated.

- Wear a scarf or muffler if it's cold out and try not to talk or inhale through your mouth when the air is terribly cold. Cold air can make your throat raw and irritated and your muscles tense.

DON'T:

- Scream and shout at sporting events or in loud bars.

- Smoke, or hang out in smoky places.

- Tackle sanding projects without a mask.

- Inhale the fumes from cleansers.

- Try a new lipstick on the day of a gig or audition—some lipsticks can cause scratchy throat or an allergic reaction.

- Clear your throat—it just makes those delicate tissues more irritated.

- If your throat is sore, don't sing. In fact, try not to talk.

- Eat/drink dairy products before singing.

- Wear perfume—you may want to ask your accompanist or anyone you're performing with to avoid perfumes too, as they can irritate the throat.

WHAT TO DO IF YOU'RE SICK

- Drink lots of warm liquids and clear broths (Tea and chicken soup—Mom was right!).
- Rest. This means stay at home and don't talk on the phone.
- Don't try to sing while your throat is inflamed. When you start singing again, take it slowly and pay attention to the way you sound and feel. If you're hoarse or if it hurts to sing, stop and wait a few more days.

SECTION **5**

Performing

CHAPTER 10
SOCIAL SINGING

What's Ahead:

- Safety in numbers
- Desperately seeking a chorus
- Follow the bouncing ball (karaoke)

Singing can be a profession, a sideline, or a hobby. No matter which it is, it's almost certainly an ongoing connection to other people who also sing.

SAFETY IN NUMBERS

The vast majority of singers in the world use their vocal abilities primarily in a chorus of some kind. Choruses range from volunteer church choirs that provide music for worship services to symphony choruses that audition for their 200-plus members and often pay a core group of singers to help lead the ensemble. In between are community choruses, men's or women's choruses, and choruses that specialize in classical music, show tunes, *early music* (European classical music written before about 1750), or even *barbershop quartet* music (close, four-part harmony sung without accompaniment, most often by men) sung by large ensembles.

Chorus options also include opera companies and troupes that perform musical theater. Both make use of choruses that appear onstage in costume. Although they're largely gone today, most large corporations in this country had choruses too, known as "corporate choruses." Still going strong in many American cities is a tradition known as the "Messiah Sing-Along," in which an orchestra and vocal soloists perform Handel's oratorio *Messiah*, with no chorus on the stage. Instead of listening to the performance, audience members bring their music and sing all of the chorus parts throughout the oratorio. Imagine the thrill of sitting in the middle of 2,000 singers performing the "Hallelujah" chorus—the sound is just unbelievable.

Photo courtesy of Andy Stenz

Bel Canto Chorus; Milwaukee, Wisconsin

Choral singing is tremendously popular in the United States. Unlike playing a band or orchestral instrument, singing doesn't take months of grueling practice to get back in shape—after all, there are no fingerings for singers to forget. Many people who sang in choral groups in high school or college take it up again years later.

Lots of choruses travel. Some set out for choral conventions, others work for years to schedule a concert tour in a place like Europe or South America. These are not paying gigs. Actually, the singers usually pay to go on these trips, but the travel expenses are low, since everything is booked as a group, and the experience of traveling and performing with friends is unforgettable.

One of the requirements of choral singing, whether in a large or small ensemble, is the ability to read choral music. In choral music, the voice parts are usually written together so that all of the singers can see how all of the voice parts fit together, no matter which part they're singing. The parts line up in logical fashion, with the soprano line on the top of the treble staff and the alto part just below it and the tenor part on the top of the bass clef with the bass part below it. The beat in both staves lines up perfectly, so that singers can see what's going on in the other parts at all times.

The staves are connected to make it easier to read the music without getting confused. Lyrics to the music are placed in between the staves in most cases.

Silent Night

Copyright © 2011 by HAL LEONARD CORPORATION
International Copyright Secured   All Rights Reserved

Words by JOSEPH MOHR
Translated by JOHN F. YOUNG
Music by FRANZ X. GRUBER

Although your rehearsals will include the entire group, or sometimes just your section in what's called a *sectional*, choral singing still requires every member to know his or her own part. Singers who can play the piano can learn the parts on their own quite easily. If you don't play the piano, or don't have one available to you, ask someone who does play to make a recording of your part for you and, if they can, have the accompaniment or the other voice parts played on piano as well. This will speed up your learning process tremendously. Choral directors often provide these recordings to group members.

Choral parts are often marked with the abbreviations S.A.T.B., denoting the soprano, alto, tenor, and bass lines respectively. Not all choral music is written for two female and two male voice parts. Singers may see music calling for S.S.A.A, or S.A.B., etc.
Choral music is almost always performed with a director, someone who is responsible for teaching the music to the singers and who also cues the group and guides them through the music in rehearsals and performance. Some choral directors use a baton to conduct, like their counterparts who conduct bands or orchestras. Others simply use hand gestures to set and keep the beat and cue the ensemble. In either case, keep your eyes on the person on the podium!

Choral singers are usually not required to memorize their music like solo performers are. Although this may sound like it would make life easier, it actually adds a challenge to whole process. As mentioned, singers in a choir are required to watch the director as they sing. Singing with music in hand requires dividing one's attention between the music and the director. At any moment, the director may also ask for one section or another to be louder or softer, or make other changes to the way they're singing their parts. It's imperative that the singers mark these instructions in their music and follow them every time they sing the piece, and then keep an eye on the director at all times in performance.

Always mark your music in pencil and always bring a couple of pencils to rehearsals. It wouldn't hurt if they had nice fresh erasers on them, too.

The other essential element in choral singing is blending with the voices around you. No chorus needs 200 soloists each vying to be the loudest, brightest, or best. Choral singers, no matter how many there are in the group, must create a unified, homogeneous sound. The choral director is the one responsible for shaping and balancing that sound, which brings us right back to the issue of writing instructions in your music and watching the director.

Most choruses have events for which they need soloists. The solos may be long or just a quick snippet of a few measures sung by a solo voice. Some choruses audition for these solo spots, giving members of the group a chance to do a little solo work. Auditioning for solos in a choral group offers singers the chance to take the spotlight without the pressure of preparing an entire solo piece.

One of the great plusses of singing in a chorus is the social interaction it provides. The moment you join a chorus, you are part of a group of people who share your interest in singing and are willing to work to create good music. What starts as a venture in choral singing can lead to lifelong friendship and unforgettable travels. Many singers belong to more than one chorus, perhaps a church group and an ensemble that gives full concerts or an opera or theater chorus. If you're thinking about joining more than one chorus, make sure their rehearsals and performances don't conflict.

Choral singing is an amazingly bonding experience. Some remarkable stories about the power of singing together came out of the terrible years of the two world wars of the 20th century.

One of the most famous such stories came from the Western Front during World War I, on Christmas Eve of 1914. As darkness fell, battle-weary German and British troops on opposite sides of a battlefield settled into their trenches to celebrate Christmas as best they could. The Germans decorated their trenches with whatever they had on hand and began singing "Stille Nacht" (Silent Night). The British troops answered, singing the carol in English. Before long the German and British troops began shouting Christmas wishes to each other across the battlefield, eventually stepping onto the field to exchange food and small items with the soldiers they had been shooting at earlier in the day. The event, which is remembered today as the "Christmas Truce," took place not just on one battlefield, but also up and down the battle lines. The Christmas Truce lasted through Christmas night at some sites, lasting through New Year's Day at other sites. In some cases it included impromptu football games between opposing forces. Many of the survivors of the war who experienced the Christmas Truce called it the most memorable Christmas of their lives.

During the second "war to end all wars" a group of Australian, Dutch, and English women were interred by the Japanese, at a prisoner-of-war camp on the island of Sumatra. For the sake of preserving morale, the women formed a chorus and sang arrangements of orchestra music prepared by one of the women in the camp. The women's story can be seen in the film *Paradise Road: Song of Survival*, starring Glenn Close, and the music can be heard on a CD of the same name, sung by the Malle Babbe Women's Chorus of Holland. The choral arrangements are gorgeous.

Some choral groups worth listening to are: Chanticleer; The King's Singers; the Robert Shaw Chorale; and the Chicago Symphony Chorus.

DESPERATELY SEEKING A CHORUS

Finding a chorus isn't difficult. Talk to singers in your area, and to voice teachers. They'll know about the various local groups and what sort of music they perform. Attend performances and see what you think of the music they perform and their performing style. Then watch the local paper for audition listings. Once you enter the choral scene in any given area, you'll find it's a pretty congenial, small world. Enjoy!

FOLLOW THE BOUNCING BALL (KARAOKE)

The latest craze in singing isn't as new as it seems. Karaoke, which is essentially a song recording in which the vocal track has been scrubbed out, or in some cases muted to a very low volume, allows wanna-be singers a chance to belt out tunes on a stage with a full back-up band. The type of Karaoke that has hit the U.S. includes a microphone and speakers to amplify both the singer and the back-up recording. Karaoke systems are appearing in more bars by the week, it seems, and finding no shortage of singers to croon a few tunes.

Karaoke became popular in Japan in the early 1970s. It spread throughout Asia during the late '70s and '80s but didn't really hit the U.S. until the 1990s. In Asia, karaoke establishments rent small rooms to parties of guests. The rooms are outfitted with karaoke machines and video equipment. Food and drink is served in the room and the karaoke sessions can be recorded as mementos of the evening. In the U.S., karaoke bars offer a much more public display. Anyone can take a high-volume shot at singing along with the sound system. A more private experience can be had by purchasing an affordable (starting at about $50) karaoke machine for the home.

Karaoke's lots of fun, as long as you pay attention to a few little details.

1. Sing a song you know. There's nothing like fumbling for notes or words to make a singer and his or her audience uncomfortable.

2. Go to a few karaoke bars before you plan to sing. Get to know the etiquette and general tone of the various places so that you feel at home there when you decide to sing.

3. Watch other karaoke singers to get your own take on what makes some singers fun to watch and others not.

4. Know your limits. If you're uncomfortable getting up in front of a large crowd, start with a small, out-of-the-way place on a quiet night. Work your way up to the larger, more crowded clubs.

5. Before you commit to singing in a karaoke bar, watch the crowd for a few minutes. Most karaoke situations are light-hearted and fun. But it only takes a couple of people at the bar to change the tone of the entire room. Listen to a couple of singers take their turns and make sure the patrons in the bar are open to karaoke fun. If not, save it for another place or evening.

Match your selection to the mood of the crowd. If things are really hopping, stay away from weepy ballads. If it's a quiet night with few patrons, an over-the-top potboiler is likely to flop. One song is plenty for starters—don't monopolize the microphone.

CHAPTER 11
LOOKING FOR WORK

What's Ahead:
- Create a résumé
- Auditions

Looking for gigs (singing jobs that pay) as a singer is unlike looking for work in most other fields. Whether you've just graduated from college with a degree in voice or you picked up this book to learn to sing, you'll go about looking for work in the same way. You are going to have to get your name and abilities in front of those who have a need for singers, and you are probably going to find yourself taking auditions.

The first step in looking for work is figuring out what type of gigs you're going after. You may be looking for work as a church soloist or chorus member. Perhaps you want to perform in some musical production (community theaters are usually more than happy to find people who can sing), or perhaps you are hoping to sing in a bar band or wedding band. Whatever kind of work you're looking for, you have to figure out who in your area does the hiring for that kind of venue and make contact with them.

CREATE A RÉSUMÉ

Some contractors or music directors will take your call and talk to you about what they are looking for and how you might audition. Others may want a résumé first and still others may want a *head shot* (the photograph singers and actors present to prospective employers) and résumé. Your musical résumé

Susan Soprano
101 Main Street
Heartland, USA 54321
Home: (888) 888-8888
Cell: (888) 888-9999
singer@internetprovider.com

OBJECTIVE
Employment as a singer

SUMMARY OF QUALIFICATIONS
Trained, versatile professional; excellent performance skills in a variety of styles; recordings and references available upon request

EXPERIENCE
Singer, 2005 to present:

Lead singer with the Indianapolis-based Going Postal country/pop band; free-lance performer with the Fort-Wayne-based Oak Leaf Big Band; paid member of the Muncie Symphony Chorus; chorus member with the Mount Pleasant Summer Dinner Theater

I specialized in parties, weddings and other events, performing jazz standards, contemporary pop, and country/pop. Can provide musical accompaniment.

EDUCATION
Private Teachers and Coaches

List names here.

ACCOLADES AND INVOLVEMENTS
Winner, Indianapolis All-City Karaoke Competition, 2008; Semi-finalist, Indiana Idol competition, 2009; Member, American Federation of Musicians, Local 9021

should be no more than one page long and should give the highlights of the singing you have done. If you don't have enough experience yet to put together a résumé, be honest about that with the person you are speaking with. They may tell you to call back when you have more experience, or may be willing to hear you audition anyway.

> A head shot should be an 8x10, black and white proof of your face, with a bit of neck and perhaps a little of your shoulders in the shot. Keep it simple. Neither a grim mug shot nor a fussy glamour shot will do. For theatre auditions, it's customary to staple your résumé to the back of your head shot, with a staple at each of the four corners. The person looking at the résumé and head shot just has to flip it over to see one or the other.

AUDITIONS

Auditions can be as different as the gigs they're set up to fill. The owner of a local bar may hire you for a single night in the bar to see how it works out. The bar owner may also want you to perform for a night for just the tips patrons are willing to give you. It's up to you how much you want the experience. A chorus director may ask you to sing a prepared number, or may just put you through a couple of scales to determine your voice category. Choruses rarely pay, although some symphony choruses and other large choirs may pay a core of singers to do extra rehearsals and help teach the music to the rest of the chorus.

Choruses in operas, operettas, and musical theater productions pay if the company is professional. A community theater production will almost undoubtedly pay nothing. But community theater productions are a low-stress way to get some performing experience and to make a circle of friends with similar interests. Auditions for this kind of chorus can vary widely. In some auditions you may be asked to sing a prepared number or two, whereas in other auditions you may be asked to read some lines or dance a few steps.

Local newspapers often run audition announcements, usually in the entertainment section and sometimes in the classifieds. Alternative weekly papers are good places to look for bands that need a singer. Voice teachers and coaches can point you toward choruses and other groups that are performing the type of music you want to sing and usually know about upcoming auditions. Talk to other singers. They know who's good to work with and who's not. The Musician's Union, the *American Federation of Musicians*, has Locals all over the country. Joining the Union in your area is good idea if your going to be working. The Union provides support for musicians and in many cases has a referral service that connects musicians to gigs.

Remember that in auditions for theatrical productions of any sort, there is the matter of "typing" to deal with. This is not a reference to the number of words one can type in a minute, but to the singer's body and face type, or "look." The director may be looking for young, tough-looking men, if casting *West Side Story*, or tall, leggy women if casting *The Producers*. You may never know what type the director of an audition is looking for, so don't be dismayed if you are "typed out," or told after a look at your head shot or body type that you're not right for the gig. It happens all the time and it's one of the reasons for the old saying: "There's a broken heart for every light on Broadway."

Tailor your audition selection to the gig you're shooting for. Don't sing a rock tune at an operetta audition and don't sing an operetta tune at a country band audition. Your teacher or coach can help you choose an appropriate song that shows off your strenths.

Don't take auditions personally. Not getting something you auditioned for does not mean that you're not a good singer. It may mean that you're tall and thin and the director was looking for someone short and round. It may mean that director already had someone in mind for the spot you were shooting for, or it may mean that they don't need you right now but will call you in the future. It could mean just about anything. Your job is to learn from the audition experience and make your next audition better and stronger.

Treat every audition like a performance. Warm up the same way you do every day. Dress appropriately for the situation. Turn off your cell phone! Hold your head high and sing to your audience, communicating with them just as though they were a paying crowd.

Break a leg!

In the theater, it's considered bad luck to wish someone "good luck." The expression "Break a leg" is used instead.

CHAPTER 12
WORKING WITH A MICROPHONE

What's Ahead:
- Details
- Hairline mics
- Studio mics

From recording studios to theater stages and from nightclubs to Karaoke clubs, working with a microphone has become an essential skill in the world of today's singer. Some microphones are no more than a tiny wire tucked into the singer's hair, while some are hand- or stand-held pieces of equipment that require some choreography to use gracefully. Knowing some basic rules for handling the various kinds of microphones is essential.

With a microphone, you can add subtle nuances or bold effects to your songs by moving the microphone closer or farther from your mouth, or pulling away from you toward the side of you face. If the microphone is stationary, mounted on a stand, you can achieve the same effects by leaning in to bring your face closer to the mic, or pulling back to move away from it. The general rule is that when you're singing softly, you want to be close to the mic so that it picks up the subtleties of the sound. When you're singing loudly, you want to back away from it a bit so that it picks up what you're doing without creating overloading and buzzing. If you're working with a stationary mic, just move your upper body as you lean in or pull back. This helps keep the changes in sound fluid and subtle. If you take a step, moving your entire body, you will probably move too far. The sudden drop or spike in sound can be more irritating than effective.

> Pay attention to singers and the way they use the microphone and how it affects their sound. Remember, you can learn from bad examples as well as good ones.

DETAILS

The letter "P" is a danger zone when working with a microphone. Singers who are not used to working with a microphone in front of them often have a hard time with the fact that a microphone picks up every detail. Those who have done mostly live theater work have the toughest time with mics. They were taught to enunciate every word so that someone sitting at the back of the hall can understand it. Such training can turn into a liability when the singer gets up-close and personal with a microphone onstage or in the studio. Those popping Ps and blasting Bs that worked so well with no microphone are absolute explosions when picked up by a mic and broadcast through a sound system. The same is true for hissing S sounds and forceful Ds and Ts. CHs don't fare so well either. Essentially, the over-enunciation of Broadway-style diction, which works well on a theater stage, has to go out the window when there's a microphone staring you in the face.

Breathing can also become an issue when working with a mic. Likewise with clearing your throat or even a gentle sniff through the nose. Remembering that the mic is live is the key to success. The mic is not only live and transmitting sound when you're singing, it's also live when you're breathing, coughing, sniffing, etc. If you're going to take an enormous breath, turn or lean away from the mic. If you're in the studio, save your throat-clearing for between takes, if at all possible. Sometimes in live performances there is no way to avoid clearing your throat or sniffling a little. If you have to make an extraneous sound, get your face as far from the mic as you can before making the sound. *Do not* try to find the switch to turn the mic off and back on again. Fumbling for the switch and then turning off and on will make an unpleasant racket when broadcast through the sound system.

The only way to learn how to work with a microphone is to actually work with one. It's best to find a way to spend some time with one in an empty studio, theater, or church where you can experiment without feeling self-conscious. Record yourself and listen critically when the session is over. Listen for popping consonants or whiny vowels that simply don't work. Also listen for the effects you thought you were making when singing into the mic. You may find that they're overdone and need to be toned down, or you may find that they're not coming through enough and need to be bolder.

Get a second set of ears involved in the learning process. Your teacher or coach may have a sound system in his or her studio that you can work with. Some vocal coaches also make "house calls," sitting in on practice sessions in theaters or studios. If your teacher or coach can't be present while you're working with a mic, they can listen to the tape you make and give you some tips and pointers.

HAIRLINE MICS

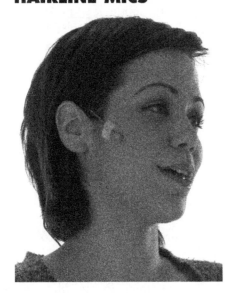

Mercifully for today's singers, microphone technology has come a long way in recent years. It wasn't that long ago that singers were saddled with body mics that picked up everything from rustling costumes to rumbling stomachs with equal clarity. The microphones used in most theaters today are known as "hairline mics," for the simple reason that they are tiny pieces of equipment worn at or near the singer's hairline. They are usually connected to a battery pack, which may or may not be easily hidden in a costume.

Hairline mics are easy to work with in that the singer basically ignores them. Since these little mics are up and away from you mouth, they won't pick up details like consonants as clearly as stationary or hand-held mics. The trick to wearing one is remembering that it's there. If you forget and reach up to scratch your head, the result can be thun-

CHAPTER 12 **WORKING WITH A MICROPHONE** **103**

derous. There's also the little matter of leaving the stage. Make sure you know how to use the volume or on/off switches on your battery pack. You don't need your backstage conversations and activities reported to an entire audience.

One of the biggest problems with hairline mics is getting them to stay in place once the wearer is perspiring under hot stage lights. If you have a problem with this, talk to the costumer or sound engineer. There are lots of tricks for keeping them in place, from a band of elastic woven through your hair to adhesives or ear clips. Not everyone has problems with this, so it will be dealt with only if you mention it.

STUDIO MICS

Studios and the equipment they use vary quite a bit. In general, you will be positioned in front of a microphone that most likely has some sort of "windscreen" in front of it. That screen is there to protect the microphone from the air and moisture that you expel as you sing. Let the sound engineer position the equipment and then DON'T TOUCH IT. First of all, it's expensive equipment. Perhaps more importantly, the sound engineer knows where he or she wants the equipment placed for the best possible results, so leave it alone. Be careful as you move about while you're singing and between takes, so that you don't bump the microphone. Again, it's expensive equipment, but it's also feeding sound into the headphones of the people in the booth. Bumping a microphone, or even just the windscreen in front of it, creates a hideous sound in their ears.

The recording engineer may outfit you with headphones too. In fact, they may be the only way for you to hear your accompaniment. The problem with this set-up is that the headphones may make it very hard for you to hear yourself. (Some headphones have a hole in the center of the portion that covers the ear. The headphone's speaker surrounds this hole, allowing the performer to hear both the recorded sound and the sound in the room.) If you are given closed headphones, you may want to try placing one of the headphones behind your ear. This allows you to hear the recorded accompaniment through one ear and the sound in the room, which includes your own sound, through the other.

CHAPTER 13
CONQUERING STAGE FRIGHT

What's Ahead:
- Nerves are not the enemy
- Beating the jitters
- Eliminating tension
- Do your homework

NERVES ARE NOT THE ENEMY

We've all seen someone step into the spotlight and freeze, with a deer-in-the-headlights look on his or her face. That's stage fright at its worst. Successful performers learn early on that the same adrenaline that causes stage fright can actually be a valuable tool—but only if it can be controlled. The adrenaline that performers experience when stepping on stage is a natural part of performing—something all performers and public speakers experience to some degree. For many musicians and other performers, that adrenaline is an essential part of getting keyed up for a gig. Adrenaline gives an edge of excitement to a performance and allows the performer to focus all of their thoughts and energy on their performance.

However, adrenaline can be a hindrance if the performer doesn't learn how to control it and channel the energy it produces. Adrenaline is a vestige of a much earlier time in human history when it triggered a flight-or-fight response that helped our forbearers survive in a hostile environment. If confronted by a bear in the wild, your adrenaline surge may help you to bolt quickly and perhaps climb a tree you otherwise might not be able to climb in order to escape. Standing in front of an audience however, neither fighting nor fleeing is going to help. So performers have to learn to deal with the physical effects of an adrenaline surge and use the sudden energy to their advantage.

BEATING THE JITTERS

Some performers are just as cool as cucumbers under pressure. They suffer no physical or mental effects of nervousness, or stage fright. Others, the minority for whom it becomes a serious problem, use hypnosis, therapy, and/or prescription drugs to minimize its effects. But the vast majority of performers fall somewhere in the middle of those two extremes: they experience some stage fright and learn to cope with nervousness and its physical effects without extreme measures.

Some of the physical signs of stage fright are a dry mouth, shaky hands or wobbly knees, cold and/or sweaty hands, a feeling of nausea, a racing heart, quivering lips. Some people also experience a momentary feeling that they've forgotten the music they're about to perform. It sounds like a dreadful list, but many of the effects of stage fright can be minimized quite easily. Avoiding caffeine and sugar in the days before a performance or the day of a performance can really help reduce jitters. Similarly, reducing salt intake can help control dry mouth problems. Alcohol, which alters the brain chemistry and dehydrates the body, should also be avoided around the time of a performance.

If you're prone to dry mouth, drink water. Many voice teachers recommend that singers start increasing water intake up to 24 hours before a performance, continuing right up to the performance. Don't eat salty foods in the couple of days leading up to a performance as this can amplify the feeling of a dry mouth and can make delicate tissues like lips and tongue retain water and feel puffy.

ELIMINATING TENSION

Most of the physical jitters that accompany nervousness are the result of tension and lack of oxygen and can be avoided pretty easily. When you're nervous you unconsciously begin taking shallow, quick breaths, robbing your body of the oxygen it needs. Lack of oxygen causes muscles to feel weak and tremble—creating wobbling knees, trembling hands, and so on. As muscles begin to tremble, the tension level rises, the breathing becomes even shallower, and the effects become even more pronounced. To nip the jitters in the bud, breathe deeply and make a conscious effort to relax your muscles, starting with neck and shoulders and progressing through muscle sets throughout your body. Remembering to take deep, easy breaths helps enormously in counteracting the physical and mental effects of nervousness.

 Keeping your muscles as relaxed as possible is also crucial to staying calm and giving an assured performance. Give your shoulders a slow gentle roll every so often, if you feel yourself getting nervous and tense. Do the same with your neck, slowly rolling your head in a complete circle, stretching and relaxing the muscles in your neck. Bend forward at the waist to touch your toes and then slowly, smoothly pull yourself back up to a standing position. This will help relax your back.

Muscle tension in the neck and shoulders often leads to tension in the arms and hands as well. If your hands are shaking or cold, let your arms and hands fall limp at your sides. Keeping your hands completely limp, begin shaking your arms around at your sides. As your hands flop back and forth limply, blood will flow back into them, warming and relaxing them.

All of the tools for mastering stage fright mentioned above take some practice to master. The best way to learn to deal with the effects of nerves is to put yourself in situations that make you nervous so that you can work on controlling those nerves. "Warm-up" performances are a great way to work some of the nerves out of a performance as you gain confidence getting up in front of an audience. The idea is to give your performance in front of an audience before the big event. The easiest way to give a warm-up performance is to gather a group of friends or neighbors and sing for them. Nursing homes are also good places for these performances. Most nursing homes have an activities director of some sort who schedules events for the residents. The experience prepares you for the ways in which your body displays nervousness and will point out what parts of your performance feel the most and least secure. Schedule the warm-up far enough in advance of the actual performance so that you have time to work on any details you might want to polish before the actual performance. Warm-up performances are such a good tool that professional singers and other musicians often perform for friends and colleagues before big performances or auditions. They get nervous too, you know.

DO YOUR HOMEWORK

Remember, a singer's job is to sing. Prepare your material well and then focus on the fact that you have a job to do. Use the warm-up exercises you do in your daily practice as you warm up for the performance. Going through these familiar warm-ups will help focus your mind on the task at hand and help prepare your body to do its best. Preparation and mental focus are your best weapons against stage fright and your best tools for giving a good performance.

CHAPTER 14
GIGGING

What's Ahead:

- The live gig
- The studio gig
- Warm up, relax, and trust yourself
- Ready, set, go...

- Applause
- Encores
- Looking ahead

THE LIVE GIG

You've practiced diligently, learned your music, scoped out performing opportunities and the big day is on the horizon—you have a gig! Following some simple rules of thumb will help you get through your first gig smoothly, as well as all those that follow.

Dress appropriately. You wouldn't show up to a formal wedding in jeans and sneakers—so don't show up to sing a wedding in those clothes either. By the same token, don't show up to sing with a bar band wearing a frilly leftover bridesmaid's dress or a tuxedo. Know the venue and occasion of your gig and then dress in clothing that makes you look professional, but that's also comfortable. Be careful not to wear anything that's too tight to let you breathe well or anything that's too revealing.

Shoes may make the man, but will almost certainly ruin the woman—at least if she's trying to stand and sing in shoes that are woefully tight or ridiculously high-heeled. Many performers keep a single pair of comfortable dress shoes that they use just for performances. The shoes a woman chooses to wear on gigs must be attractive, supportive, stable, and comfortable. If you're wobbling on your shoes, you can't possibly be breathing and supporting well.

Choose the clothing you plan to wear a day or two ahead of time so that you avoid the "What am I going to wear?" crisis on gig day, or perhaps worse, the "Where are my good shoes?" panic. Treat your gig clothing like a costume, which means no eating or drinking while wearing it. You may be wearing your best suit and tie, but slopping coffee on the front of it while driving to the gig will kill your chances of looking professional. If you have to eat on your way to the gig, wear something else and carry your gig clothing on a hanger.

Before you set out for your gig, double- and triple-check that you have everything you need to perform well. Check for your music and the music for your accompanist, if you need to provide it. Make sure you have a bottle of water. The possibilities of dust in the balcony of a church, smoke in a nightclub or bar, or the perfume of your accompanist setting off an allergy event are great—bring tissues and lozenges. If you use an inhaler or some sort of allergy medication, bring it as well. You can't be too careful when you're performing.

Before the big day arrives, check that you have directions to the venue as well as a contact phone number and the correct time of the gig. Always allow time for traffic problems and the possibility of getting lost. It's always better to arrive with a little extra warm-up time than to run in at the last minute, or worse, late.

> If you're not at least 30 minutes early for a gig, you're late!

You may find yourself in the position of traveling far enough for your gig that you need to spend the night away from home. If so, you'll have to do your check and double-check twice: once before you leave home to travel and once before you leave your hotel for the gig.

> Airlines lose luggage. Always take your performing clothes, shoes, cosmetics, and all your music—essentially, everything you need to do the gig—on the plane with you to ensure that it will arrive with you.

THE STUDIO GIG

Studio work is a world away from live performance and, in a way, more difficult. On a live gig, a slightly sharp note or a slightly late entrance is over the moment it happens. Your audience isn't likely to notice a small flaw here or there. But on a studio gig, it's all about perfection. Your performance will be replayed and double-checked to make sure everything is in place.

In studio work, time is money. The time spent in a studio with a producer and a sound engineer, and possibly backup musicians, is very expensive. If you want to do studio work, you need to be extremely prepared for each gig. You don't want to be the reason for multiple takes of the material. You don't want to be the reason for any delays. Arrive early and arrive already warmed up. Bring a bottle of water, a snack if you feel you might need one. If it's a long session, there will be breaks and the snack may help you keep your energy up. Make sure the snack isn't messy and that you take any wrappers or other refuse with you. Never, *ever* put liquids or food on speakers, recording consoles, or musical instruments.

Preparing for studio work involves learning your music and possibly taking it to a coach. Studios are the one place where memorization is never required. In fact, most producers will want you to have the music on hand so that you can mark any changes or suggestions that are given to you. Even though you don't need to have it memorized, it's not a bad idea to memorize it anyway – or at least be familiar enough with it so that you don't have to keep your nose buried in the music for the entire session.

Pay attention to the folks in the booth as you sing. Sometimes you can avoid a retake by responding on the fly to what they want you to do—like slowing down a bit or making a line more expressive. Remember that the recording engineer does not necessarily stop taping the moment you stop singing. Don't talk or make sounds until you know the tape is no longer rolling.

One of the most difficult things about recording gigs is that you have to stand alone in a studio and muster the same energy you feel when you step out in front of an audience. This fact alone can make recording sessions exhausting. When most singers perform onstage, they use facial expressions and hand gestures to help communicate with their audience. Feel free to use these devices in the recording studio as well. Most singers and voice-over artists are very animated as they tape their work. Those facial gestures and other movements that you would use in live performance help bring excitement, energy, and emotion to your voice.

Be professional, be pleasant, be flexible, and don't be a diva. Some of the finest, most famous singers in the world have lost work by being difficult.

> Make certain you dress in layered clothing for studio gigs. Studios can be very dry and over-air-conditioned, or terribly warm and stuffy. Either way, having layers of clothing that you can put on or take off easily will help you stay comfortable and do your best.

WARM UP, RELAX, AND TRUST YOURSELF

Warm up at home on the day of the gig. You will want to do another warm-up, perhaps a little shorter one, at the venue, but you'll warm up more thoroughly at home, without whatever distractions the venue offers. Don't over sing. You want to warm up just enough so that your voice is limber and responding as you want it to. You may want to start and end the song (or songs) with your accompanist or band members, just for the sake of security. But you definitely do not want to run through all the songs you are planning to sing, as you're warming up for the gig.

You want to sound fresh and well-rested, not tired from having sung too much. Some professional singers won't even speak for 24 or 48 hours before a gig or recording date. You don't need to go that far, unless you've landed some huge role in a four-hour opera, but you do need to be aware of keeping your voice in good shape for a gig. No smoking or drinking alcohol in the days leading up to a gig. It's best to avoid smoky situations entirely in the days before a gig. No shouting or screaming at sporting events in the days before a gig. Crying is also hard on the voice, so avoid sad books and films in the days before the gig. Rest your voice as much as possible and keep it hydrated—drink lots of water.

READY, SET, GO...

In the last moments before you sing, you should be breathing deeply and relaxing as much as possible. Keep your body relaxed by rolling your shoulders, shaking out your arms and hands and stretching a bit before you step in front of your audience (See Chapter 4 for some useful relaxation exercises.)

 TURN OFF YOUR CELL PHONE! Yours is the one cell phone in the room that simply cannot ring during your performance. Turn it off before you go onstage, then check it at least once to make sure it's off and do *not* it take it onstage with you.

Here's where running through songs from top to bottom without stops comes in handy. You cannot stop a song once you've begun it when you're onstage. You have to be prepared to soldier on even if you miss a note, come in early or late on an entrance or forget some lyrics. The show, as the old theater saying goes, must go on.

As you step in front of your audience, remember to smile, stand up straight, and connect with the people who are there to listen to you. Your stage presence matters.

APPLAUSE

Singers must be able to accept applause gracefully. That may mean smiling and nodding your head in acknowledgement, or it may mean a full-fledged bow. Practice these gestures in front of a mirror to make sure you are moving elegantly. Women, remember what you're wearing: a low-cut dress becomes distinctly lower as you bow.

When people compliment your performance, it's your job to be gracious. Don't tell them what went wrong, or complain about the drafty stage or out-of-tune piano you had to deal with. Smile and thank them for their kind words.

If you're in a situation where you leave the stage and the audience is still applauding vigorously, count to three and step back out on the stage to take another bow. If the applause is beginning to die down, stay off the stage. You don't want to appear hungry for the applause by striding out onstage when the audience is not actually calling for it.

Always assume the microphone is on—particularly a microphone you're wearing. Be very careful not to start talking, sighing, or making other noises as you walk off the stage. Otherwise you may end up broadcasting that sound to your audience.

ENCORES

In some situations you may be called upon to give an encore, which amounts to an additional, brief number that is not included in the body of your performance. An encore (which, by the way, means "more" in Italian) is an answer to enthusiastic applause. You should be flattered if this occurs, because it means the audience wants to hear more of your singing. Unfortunately, encores are like umbrellas: you seem to need one only if you don't have one. Always make sure you have an encore ready, which means having both the music for yourself and for your accompanist on hand and making sure you've rehearsed it a few times for good measure. You never want to be in the position of giving a lovely performance and then falling apart during your encore.

LOOKING AHEAD

Music is very often a word-of-mouth business. Many musicians view each performance as an audition for future performances. If you sing well at one wedding, the church organist or wedding planner may recommend you for upcoming weddings. The same goes for any gig you sing—if you do a good job, it may lead to more work. But bad news always travels faster than good news. If you are too ill to sing well, find someone to fill in for you. In short, always be professional about the way you handle gigs, and you will find more and more of them coming your way.

Enjoy yourself. Singing is one of life's great pleasures!

Reading Music – The Basics

CHAPTER 15
GETTING STARTED

What's Ahead:
- A universal language
- Time for a rest
- The ties that bind
- Name that note
- Telling time

If you take ten people, tell a short story to one of them and then have each of them tell the next person until the story comes back to you, you'll end up with a wildly altered story. The reason for the disparity between the first and last versions of the story is that they each had to learn the story without having read it. They had to rely on what they heard and what they remembered as they repeated the story to the next person.

Music is no different. If you can't read music, you have no way of knowing if you're singing what the composer wrote, or if you're really singing someone else's recollection or interpretation of the song. The ability to read music is as freeing as the ability to read words. If you had to seek out a reader every time you needed to understand instructions or directions, you'd be terribly limited. The same is true in music. You're limiting yourself by not learning to read music.

Reading music means more than knowing that the melody goes up when the notes go uphill. It means learning to connect written music to the magical combination of rhythm and sound that makes each piece of music a unique musical experience. It's not a great mystery! Young children learn to read music, just as young children learn to read words. Like any new skill, it has to be learned in bits, every piece of knowledge building upon the last.

Once you can read music fluently, you'll be free of the need to have an accompanist teach you songs or to have to find recordings to learn from. You'll be able to make your own decisions about interpreting the music you're working on, without relying on what someone else did with the song before you. In short, you'll be a far more creative, competent singer.

A UNIVERSAL LANGUAGE

Written music is a language that's read throughout the world. All musicians read the same music, no matter where they live or what language they speak. Within the language of music are several terms that are words borrowed from other languages, but these too are universal. "Allegro" means a quick tempo in all corners of the world. At the end of the book you'll find a section on the terms you're most likely to see in printed music (and their abbreviations, if there are any). For now, we'll get you started reading basic music notation.

In order to understand how written music works, you must first understand that every note in a piece of music tells a musician two very important things: what sound to make, or the *pitch* of a note, and how long to make that sound, or the *rhythm* of the note. Other details, like how fast the piece should go, its *tempo*, and how loudly or softly the notes should be played or sung, the *dynamics* of the piece, are also indicated in printed music, by symbols that are explained in Chapter 7 (Making Music). But pitch and rhythm are equally important parts of the basis of any music making. You simply have to hit the right notes at the right time before you begin to worry about anything else.

But first things first! Every time you hear a piece of music and find yourself tapping your foot along with it, you are tapping the beat of the music. The way each note is written tells you how many beats, or fractions of a beat, that particular note will take up.

A whole note is four beats long.

A half note is two beats long.

A quarter note is one beat long.

When we count quarter note, half note, and whole note rhythms out loud, we use the syllable "tah" for each quarter note. Half notes are counted "ta-ah," with just a slight accent on the "ah." Whole notes are counted "tah-ah-ah-ah," with just slight accents on the "ah" syllables.

Whole notes are four beats long.

Half notes are two beats long.

Quarter notes are one beat long.

Now listen to Track 35, the sound of a steady beat. Try counting the following rhythms aloud using the syllables you learned above. Don't worry if you have trouble staying with the metronome at first—it's a skill that takes time to develop. Keep working at it, just like you did with the long lines of "Amazing Grace."

The clicking sound you hear in Track 35 is a device known as a metronome. These little time-keepers give musicians a steady beat for practicing.

There's one more addition to the basic family of notes that you will need to know in order to get started: the dotted half notes. Placing a dot beside a note increases the value of that note by one half. So, if you place a dot beside a half note, it adds one beat, making the note three beats long.

Try the following counting exercises using the metronome beat in Track 35. Listen to Track 36 to check yourself.

It may be very helpful to write in the beats—using numbers, as in the previous examples—as you're learning a piece of music. Until you're certain of the rhythm, you might also find it useful to practice the piece without words, singing the counting numbers or syllables instead of the lyrics.

TIME FOR A REST

Just as important to the rhythm of a piece as the rhythm of the notes is the rhythm of the occasional silent space between the notes. As you work on the songs included in the book, you'll start to appreciate those rests—often, they give you time to get a good breath!

Rests have to be counted just as carefully as the notes themselves. Just as notes come in whole, half, and quarter varieties, so do rests.

The whole rest is four beats long:

The half rest is two beats long:

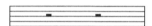

The quarter rest is one beat long:

Listen to the following examples in Track 37 of the CD and then try counting them yourself.

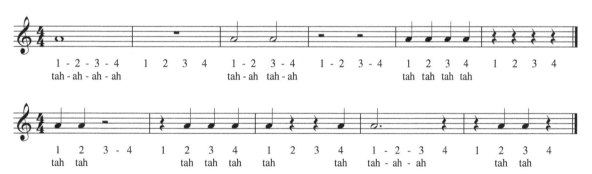

THE TIES THAT BIND

You've learned to read whole notes, half notes, dotted half notes, and quarter notes. Sometimes in music, a bar line will get in the way of using a half, dotted-half, or whole note to indicate a long note. In that case, you may see a "tie," a curved line connecting two note notes. A tie is the musical equivalent of a plus sign. You add the two notes together to create one longer note.

NAME THAT NOTE

Now that we've tackled the basics of rhythm, let's look at pitch. Music is written on what is called a staff, a set of five parallel lines.

Not all notes fit neatly on the staff, so extensions called ledger lines are sometimes used.

At the beginning of each staff in a piece of music is a symbol called a clef. In vocal music, and in the keyboard parts that often accompany vocal music, you are likely to find two clefs: the treble clef and the bass clef.

TREBLE CLEF

BASS CLEF

The clef is the symbol that tells you the pitch and name of the note. Notes have one set of names if there's a treble clef at the beginning of the staff and another set of names if there's bass clef there. Learning the names of the notes is not difficult. There are only seven note names to worry about: A, B, C, D, E, F, G. Once you get to G, you start over again with A.

A treble clef indicates that notes are positioned on the following lines and spaces:

For some people, assigning words to the notes helps in remembering how they line up. Needless to say, it won't take long before you'll be reading along without the mnemonic device. Notes in the treble clef can be remembered with simple phrases in which each word starts with the same letter as the note name. The following examples show you how to remember the notes names for notes that fall on lines in the staff, and for notes that fall on spaces in the staff.

In bass clef, the lines and spaces take different note names than treble clef.

Here too, assigning words to the notes may help as your first learning.

Pieces of music are divided into *measures*, or *bars*, all of which contain the same number of beats. Measures are separated by little vertical lines called *bar lines*.

TELLING TIME

At the beginning of a piece of music, the clef is always followed by a *time signature*, which looks like a fraction missing the line that divides the two numbers. The time signature indicates the meter of a piece. When someone says a piece is "in 3," or "in 4," they are referring to the meter defined by the time signature.

Basic time signatures are pretty easy to read. The top number indicates how many notes are in each measure, while the bottom number indicates what kind of notes make up the beats in each measure.

Four beats in each measure, each beat is a quarter note.

Three beats in each measure, each beat is a quarter note.

Time signatures also occur in music whenever the time signature of a piece changes.

Four-four time is also known as "common time" and is sometimes indicated with a C in place of the time signature.

So let's give these new skills a try. The song "Hey Lolly, Lolly," is constructed of quarter notes and half notes. The song originated in Jamaica, as part of the calypso tradition. Calypso music began to appear around 1900 in the Caribbean, where African slaves, who weren't allowed to talk to each other as they worked, would sing together.

The song ranges from a D to an A, and is constructed of quarter notes and half notes. The singer on the CD will sing through the song using the note names instead of words. Then the singer will sing the melody, using the beat names instead of words. Listen to the singer and follow the song in the book. Feel free to write in the note names above the notes, or the counting below the notes, if it helps you get used to reading this new language.

Hey Lolly, Lolly

Copyright © 2000 by HAL LEONARD CORPORATION
International Copyright Secured All Rights Reserved

Jamaican Calypso

1. Mar - ried   men   will   keep   your   se - cret.
2. Two   old   maids   sit - tin'   in   the   sand.
3. I   have   a   girl,   she's   ten   foot   tall.
4. Ev - 'ry - bod - y   sing   the   cho - rus.

Hey   lol - ly,   lol - ly   lo.

Sin - gle   boys   will   talk   a - bout   you.
Each   one   wish - in'   the   oth - er   was   a   man.
Sleeps   in   the   kitch - en   with her   feet   in   the   hall.
Ei - ther you're   for   us   or   a - gainst   us.

Hey   lol - ly,   lol - ly   lo.

Hey   lol - ly,   lol - ly,   lol - ly,   hey   lol - ly,   lol - ly,   lo.

Hey   lol - ly,   lol - ly,   lol - ly,   hey   lol - ly,   lol - ly   lo.

Now the singers will perform the song with the lyrics. Listen, while watching the music, a couple of times and then sing along. Use Track 41 to try all these ways of singing it—on your own!

Always look ahead as you read music. Make sure your eyes are at least a couple of beats ahead of the note you're singing so that there are no surprises waiting for you. As a rule, surprises create mistakes.

Now take a look at the following songs: "The Way You Look Tonight," "I Could Have Danced All Night," and "There's No Business Like Show Business." They are included here for your further study. Use the skills you learned in this chapter to learn the songs.

To work on your counting skills, write in the counting (in pencil) and sing the songs through with the counting syllables. Then do the same with the note names. If you go through these steps each time you work on a song, your music reading skills will improve very quickly. Once you have learned the music, look for the recordings and films that made these songs famous. The performers will each bring their own unique sense of style and their own personal experiences to their interpretations.

"The Way You Look Tonight" received an Academy Award for Best Original Song in 1936, after Fred Astaire sang it in the film *Swing Time*. It is constructed of quarter notes, half notes and whole notes. The melody of this song was written by Jerome Kern, who wrote more than 700 songs in his lifetime, including those for the musical *Show Boat*. Dorothy Fields, who once said that this melody brought tears to her eyes when Kern first played it for her, wrote the lyrics. Additional recordings by Michael Bublé and Tony Bennett are well worth listening to.

The song "Lover" first appeared in the 1932 film *Love Me Tonight*, where Jeanette MacDonald sang it—on horseback. The song was written by Richard Rodgers and Lorenz Hart, the team that produced classic songs like "Bewitched" and "Manhattan," as well as musicals such as *On Your Toes*. For a number of different interpretations of "Lover," listen to recordings by Peggy Lee, the Supremes, Frank Sinatra (the 1950 recording), and Joni James.

The Way You Look Tonight
from SWING TIME

Words by DOROTHY FIELDS
Music by JEROME KERN

Copyright © 1936 UNIVERSAL - POLYGRAM INTERNATIONAL PUBLISHING, INC. and ALDI MUSIC
Copyright Renewed
Print Rights for ALDI MUSIC in the U.S. Controlled and Administered by HAPPY ASPEN MUSIC LLC c/o SHAPIRO, BERNSTEIN & CO., INC.
All Rights Reserved   Used by Permission

Lover
from the Paramount Picture LOVE ME TONIGHT

Words by LORENZ HART
Music by RICHARD RODGERS

Copyright © 1932 Sony/ATV Music Publishing LLC
Copyright Renewed
All Rights Administered by Sony/ATV Music Publishing LLC, 8 Music Square West, Nashville, TN 37203
International Copyright Secured   All Rights Reserved

Congratulations! You have learned the basics of music reading. Later in the book you'll learn more about the symbols and words that are often used in music to give additional directions to musicians. But for now, you have the tools to begin finding your voice and reading some basic music.

Here's another song to test your new skills, "There's No Business Like Show Business," from the musical *Annie Get Your Gun*. Irving Berlin wrote the words and music to this gem of a song—the same man who gave us such classics as "God Bless America" and "White Christmas." Although "There's No Business Like Show Business" was sung by company members in the musical *Annie Get You Gun*, it became Ethel Merman's signature song. Rosemary Clooney also sang a memorable version.

Again, to work on your counting skills, write in the beats (in pencil) and sing it through with the counting syllables. Then do the same with the note names. If you go through these steps each time you work on a song, your music reading skills will improve very quickly.

Notice that in each recording you study, the singer takes his or her own liberties with tempo, and sometimes with rhythm, in their interpretations of the songs. You have the freedom to take interpretive liberties with the songs too, but before you can do that you have to learn the song as it was written. Use the tools you've acquired in this chapter to learn the songs and then have fun as you begin to make them your own.

There's No Business Like Show Business.

from the Stage Production ANNIE GET YOUR GUN

Words and Music by
IRVING BERLIN

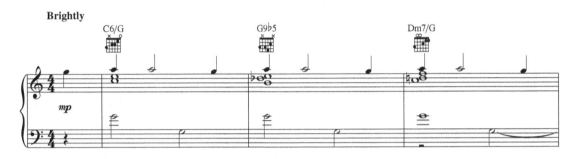

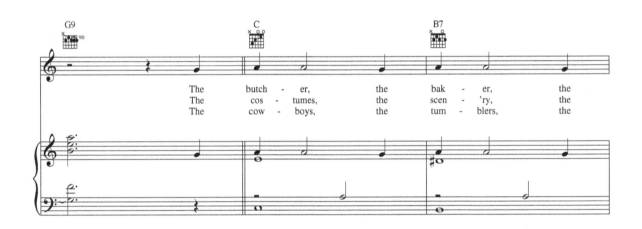

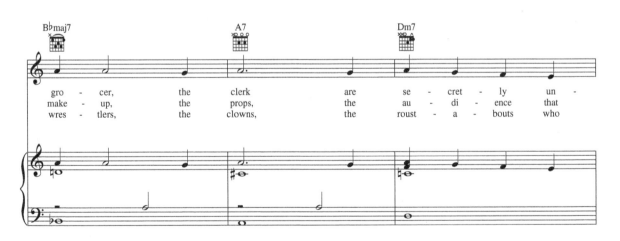

© Copyright 1946 by Irving Berlin
Copyright Renewed
International Copyright Secured   All Rights Reserved

CHAPTER 16
YOU'VE GOT RHYTHM

What's Ahead:

- Subdivisions and more dots
- In triplicate
- And all that jazz
- Cut time
- Yet more dots
- Time warp

SUBDIVISIONS AND MORE DOTS

Notes can also be subdivided to give a sense of energy and motion to a piece of music. Just as whole notes can be divided into two half notes or four quarter notes, quarter notes can be divided into two eighth notes or into four 16th notes.

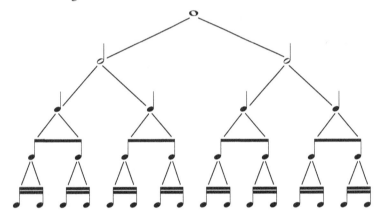

When you're learning a song that contains eighth notes and 16th notes, it helps to count them carefully. We sang through "Hey Lolly, Lolly" (page 117) singing the beat names instead of the lyrics. We can sing through a song with eighths and 16ths in the same way.

Remember that a dot placed beside a note adds half again the value of that note? The same is true if the note is a quarter note, in which case the dot adds the value of an eighth note to create a note that is one-and-a-half beats long.

Listen to the singer on the CD perform "Danny Boy," using the rhythm syllables. Read along with the music. Once you're comfortable with the counting, try to sing along. Now try singing the rhythm syllables to the accompaniment on Track 44. (A performance with the lyrics is on Track 43.)

Danny Boy

Words by FREDERICK EDWARD WEATHERLY
Traditional Irish Folk Melody

Copyright © 1993 by HAL LEONARD CORPORATION
International Copyright Secured All Rights Reserved

Now listen to the singer perform the song with the lyrics. Read along in the music. When you are comfortable with the lyrics, sing along. Then try singing along to accompaniment in Track 44. "Danny Boy" is actually the Irish folk melody "Londonderry Air." The lyrics were written by Frederick Weatherly in about 1910. He wrote them to a different tune, but when he heard "Londonderry Air," he reworked the words to fit this lovely melody. It became one of the most popular songs of the early 20th century and remains a standard in Celtic music today.

IN TRIPLICATE

You've learned to divide quarter notes into pairs of eighth notes, so it's time to try your hand at triplets. Triplets are just what the name implies, divisions of a single beat into three equal parts. Music teachers love to offer up words that help students hear the triplet as three even notes, English words that are spoken as triplets, like: elephant, butterfly, violin, or bumbershoot, if you happen to be British.

Track 45 on the CD will give you several triplet beats in a row, with an accent on the beginning of the triplet. Speak the "triplet words" above with the triplets on the recording, keeping them nice and even.

Track 46 will give you a vocal exercise in triplets. Sing the words above with the exercise, using one word for the entire exercise. Select the word that feels the most natural for you and use that word to keep your triplets even as you learn songs like "What'll I Do." Make sure that the triplet on the words "what'll I" is actually a triplet and not a combination of an eighth and two sixteenths. Use one of the above words to check yourself.

The song "What'll I Do?" is a great example of a standard that has never left popular culture. Written in 1923 by Irving Berlin, it was introduced that year in a production called *Music Box Revue*. The melancholy song wonders how the singer is going to cope with the end of a relationship. It has been recorded over the years by such artists as Cher, Art Garfunkel, Lena Horne, Johnny Mathis, Anne Murray, Frank Sinatra, Sarah Vaughan and a host of others. An instrumental version of the wistful melody was heard on the TV series *Cheers*, at the end of the relationship between Sam and Diane.

What'll I Do?

from MUSIC BOX REVUE OF 1924

Words and Music by
IRVING BERLIN

© Copyright 1924 by Irving Berlin
© Arrangement Copyright 1947 by Irving Berlin
Copyright Renewed
International Copyright Secured All Rights Reserved

Now try singing the song with the accompaniment on track 48. Repeat it until you're comfortable with the triplets.

AND ALL THAT JAZZ

Some music just gets under one's skin. There's something about the rhythm that's particularly fascinating. The rhythm is probably syncopated, which means that the notes don't fall neatly on the beats. The result grabs the attention of the listener.

At the end of Chapter 1, you worked on the song "Sometimes I Feel Like a Motherless Child." You learned it by listening to the singer on the CD. Here's a chance to look at it again, this time reading the notes instead of depending on someone else's performance to learn and understand it. The more you can rely on your own music reading skills to learn songs, the more quickly you will form your own interpretations of those songs.

Notice that the second notes of the first, third, and fifth measures have a syncopated feel to them. Also notice the triplet over two beats that occurs in measures two, four, and six. There are syncopations in each of those six measures. The piano accompaniment is on Track 49.

As you learn the following song, the standard "Stormy Weather," written by Ted Koehler and Harold Arlen, pay close attention to the rhythms. In addition to some generally interesting dotted rhythms and triplets, there is a wonderful syncopated rhythm in the phrase "keeps rainin' all the time." The syncopation falls on the word "all." Also notice that the triplets are either tied to the note that follows or to the preceding note, creating more syncopations. Don't forget to listen to several recordings of the song. It's been recorded by Lena Horne, Billie Holiday, and by Ella Fitzgerald with guitarist Joe Pass.

Stormy Weather
(Keeps Rainin' All the Time)
from COTTON CLUB PARADE OF 1933

Lyric by TED KOEHLER
Music by HAROLD ARLEN

© 1933 (Renewed 1961) FRED AHLERT MUSIC GROUP (ASCAP), TED KOEHLER MUSIC CO. (ASCAP)/Administered by BUG MUSIC and S.A. MUSIC CO.
All Rights Reserved   Used by Permission

CUT TIME

Sometimes things just need to move quickly. When that's the case, you may find a curious symbol in place of the time signature in your music. The symbol, a C with a vertical line running through it, indicates "cut time," or "alla breve." It means that instead of counting the measures in four, which is what they look like, you count them in two. You place beats on the first and third quarter note of each bar. This makes it easier, from a counting perspective, to take the piece up to the desired tempo.

 Listen to the singer on Track 50 performing a familiar 19th Century tune from the American West, "She'll Be Comin' 'Round the Mountain."

She'll Be Comin' 'Round the Mountain

Copyright © 2000 by HAL LEONARD CORPORATION
International Copyright Secured   All Rights Reserved

Traditional

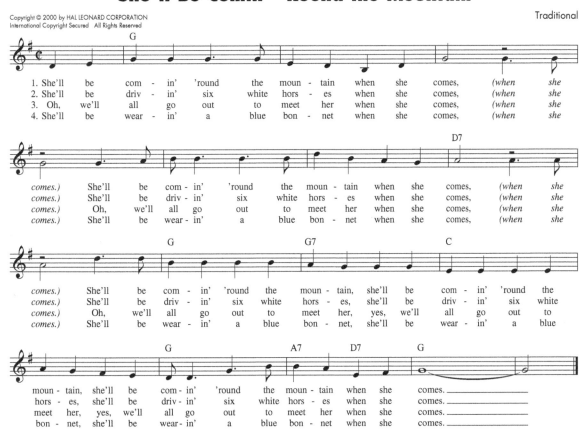

Notice that the cut-time feel of the song gives it energy and momentum? Try singing it on your own with accompaniment in Track 51.

The following song, "California Dreamin'," was written by John and Michelle Phillips and scored a hit for their group, the Mamas & the Papas, in 1965. Find a recording of the group performing the song and clap along with the beats as you listen. Listen again and clap along with the melody. Clapping the beats and clapping the rhythms is always a good way to ensure that you are leaning correct rhythms right from the beginning.

> It's always better to learn music correctly in the first place, rather than putting yourself in the position of have to unlearn and relearn it.

California Dreamin'

Words and Music by JOHN PHILLIPS
and MICHELLE PHILLIPS

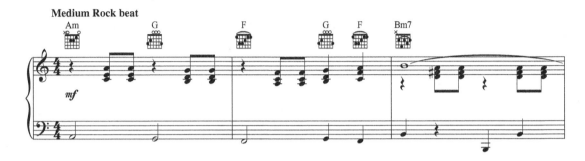

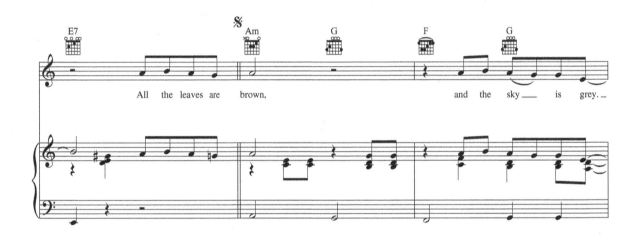

Copyright © 1965 UNIVERSAL MUSIC CORP.
Copyright Renewed
All Rights Reserved   Used by Permission

YET MORE DOTS

Just when you thought you were done with dots, you have a few more to learn about. You can add dots to eighth notes and 16th notes, too. When you add dots to notes that are already pretty short, you create a lilting feel in the music.

Listen to the singer in Track 52 perform Robert Lowry's 19th Century American hymn tune, "Shall We Gather at the River." Notice that the measures with the dotted-eighth/sixteenth rhythm have a little lilt. They remind one a bit of the motion of a small boat on water. Try it for yourself, using the piano part on Track 53.

Jerry Lieber and Mike Stoller's rhythm and blues tune "Kansas City" is a great example of the energy dotted rhythms can bring to a melody as well as the way in which performers like to interpret such rhythms. A video of a fairly early Beatles performance of "Kansas City" and another of Fats Domino performing the songs provide good opportunities to follow the music while listening to the song.

Kansas City

Words and Music by JERRY LEIBER
and MIKE STOLLER

I'm go-in' to Kan-sas Cit-y,___ Kan-sas Cit-y here I come.___

I'm go-in' to Kan-sas Cit-y,___ Kan-sas Cit-y here I come.___

They got a

Copyright © 1952 Sony/ATV Music Publishing LLC
Copyright Renewed
All Rights Administered by Sony/ATV Music Publishing LLC, 8 Music Square West, Nashville, TN 37203
International Copyright Secured   All Rights Reserved

TIME WARP

Thus far, every time signature you've seen has had a four as the bottom number, meaning that beats in the measures were the value of quarter notes. That's not always the case. Another very common time signature is 6/8.

$$\frac{6}{8}$$

Since the top number tells us how many beats are in each measure and the bottom number tells us the value of those beats, we know that each 6/8 measure will have six beats in it, and each one will have the value of an eighth note. The eighth notes are usually grouped in threes, in 6/8 time, making each beat feel like an even triplet.

Listen to the singer in Track 54 singing John Lennon and Paul McCartney's "You've Got to Hide Your Love Away," which was one of the many British and American hits charted by the Beatles. Watch the music and pay attention to the syncopations created on the words "hide your love."

You've Got to Hide Your Love Away

Words and Music by JOHN LENNON
and PAUL McCARTNEY

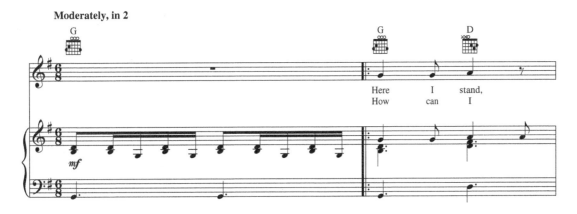

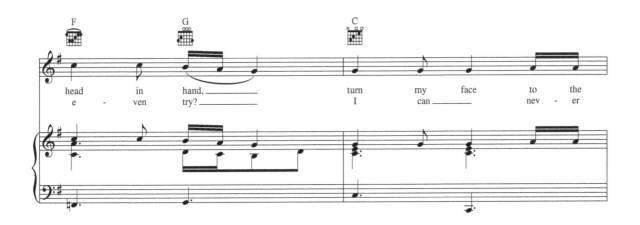

Copyright © 1965 Sony/ATV Music Publishing LLC
Copyright Renewed
All Rights Administered by Sony/ATV Music Publishing LLC, 8 Music Square West, Nashville, TN 37203
International Copyright Secured All Rights Reserved

Now sing it alone with the accompaniment in Track 55. Make sure your groups of three eighth notes are even and your dotted rhythms gentle and flowing.

Your music reading skills are growing by the chapter. As you listen to music, on the radio, on your iPod or MP3, in film scores, or even just in television commercials, make a point to listen closely. Tap your foot and see if you can tell whether something is in 4/4, cut-time, 3/4, or 6/8. There are other time signatures, but the ones you have learned so far are the most common.

Here are two songs on which you can try out your growing music reading skills. The first one is Lennon and McCartney's nostalgic "In My Life." The Beatles released this song on their 1965 *Rubber Soul* album. Look for additional recordings of "In My Life" by such artists as the Beatles and Bette Midler.

The second song, "Unforgettable," was written by Irving Gordon. Nat King Cole's 1951 recording of this lyrical song really *is* unforgettable. His daughter, Natalie Cole, charted with the same song in 1991, performing it as a duet with her father, using her father's original recording from 40 years earlier. Look for the recording of "Unforgettable" by Nat King Cole, Natalie Cole, or perhaps the unforgettable recording of the two of them singing it together through the wonders of recording technology.

Always do some homework on the songs you're singing. You need to know who wrote each one—and when—in order to do them justice.

In My Life

Words and Music by JOHN LENNON
and PAUL McCARTNEY

Copyright © 1965 Sony/ATV Music Publishing LLC
Copyright Renewed
All Rights Administered by Sony/ATV Music Publishing LLC, 8 Music Square West, Nashville, TN 37203
International Copyright Secured   All Rights Reserved

Unforgettable

Words and Music by
IRVING GORDON

Copyright © 1951 by Bourne Co. (ASCAP)
Copyright Renewed
International Copyright Secured   All Rights Reserved

CHAPTER 17
KEYS, SCALES, AND FORMS

What's Ahead:

- Symbols and their meanings
- Key signatures
- Major and minor scales
- Modes
- Road maps
- Changes in key signatures
- Transposing
- Using your new skills

SYMBOLS AND THEIR MEANINGS

You've learned how to read notes and rhythms and time signatures. There's just one big element of music left for you to tackle: key signatures. In order to understand sharps, flats, and key signatures, you have to understand that music moves up and down in steps. We call the steps whole steps and half steps.

Look at the keyboard below, and notice that between the C and D keys there's a black key that's labeled C♯/D♭. The interval, or distance, from C to D is one whole step. In between the two notes are two half steps: one from C to C♯/D♭ and one from C♯/D♭ to D.

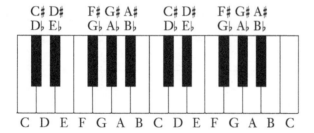

If you go up or down the keyboard hitting every half step, or every note possible, you create what's known as a chromatic scale. The word chromatic comes from the Greek language, where it means "color."

When sharps or flats appear right before a note in a piece of music, we call them accidentals. They are there to raise or lower the note they sit beside by one half step.

Look at the song, "Beautiful Dreamer" by Stephen Foster, who is remembered as the "Father of American Popular Music." He lived from 1826 to 1864, and began writing popular songs at a time when Americans were still relying on songs brought from Europe. Although he died in poverty, we've never stopped singing his songs.

Notice the chromatic note (the accidental) in measures 2, 6, and 14. Listen to the singer in Track 56. Sing the song and pay attention to the color those accidentals bring to the piece. The piano part is on Track 57.

Look at the song, "Wake Up, Little Susie." Look for recordings of the song by the Everly Brothers or a later recording by Paul Simon and Art Garfunkel. Listen to the singers, watch the music, and pay attention to the color those accidentals bring to the piece. The Everly Brothers popularized this song, taking it to the top of the pop charts in 1957. Even so, it was banned in Boston, because of "suggestive" lyrics.

Wake Up, Little Susie

Words and Music by BOUDLEAUX BRYANT
and FELICE BRYANT

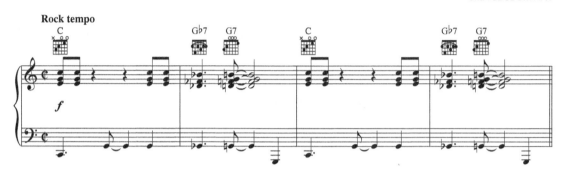

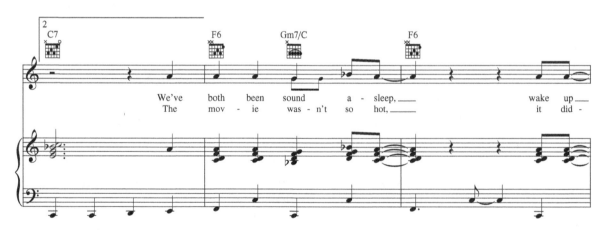

Copyright © 1957 by HOUSE OF BRYANT PUBLICATIONS, Gatlinburg, TN
Copyright Renewed
All Foreign Rights Controlled by SONY/ATV MUSIC PUBLISHING LLC
All Rights on behalf of SONY/ATV MUSIC PUBLISHING LLC Administered by SONY/ATV MUSIC PUBLISHING LLC, 8 Music Square West, Nashville, TN 37203
International Copyright Secured   All Rights Reserved

Three other accidentals may pop up in pieces of music: the natural, which sits right in front of a note to tell you to cancel whatever sharp or flat sign was affecting the note in the first place; the natural, which tells you cancel out a sharp or flat that may be affecting the note it sits beside; the double flat, which tells you lower the note it's sitting beside by two half steps; and the double sharp, which tells you to raise the note it's sitting beside by one half step.

Natural

Double Flat

Double Sharp

KEY SIGNATURES

When sharps and flats appear in between the clef and the time signature, we call them a key signature.

Flats in Key Signature

Sharps in Key Signature

Here are the key signatures for all the major and minor scales:

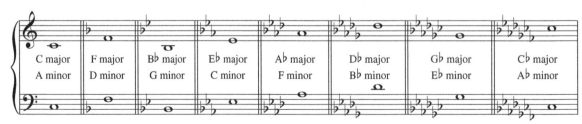

MAJOR AND MINOR SCALES

The name of the key signature indicates the starting note of the scale created by that key signature. In a major scale, the key signature lines up the whole steps and half steps to create a bright, rather happy sounding scale.

Major Scale

Listen to the singer in Track 58 sing the German song "Let Us All Be Joyful Now" (Gaudeamus Igitur). Notice the solid, happy feel of the key. Dating from the 13th century, the lighthearted song is one of many academic "commercium" songs that were once part of European university life. It is still the official song of many modern academic institutions. Johannes Brahms incorporated the tune into his *Academic Festival Overture*.

Let Us All Be Joyful Now
(Gaudeamus Igitur)

Copyright © 2000 by HAL LEONARD CORPORATION
International Copyright Secured   All Rights Reserved

German Student Drinking Song

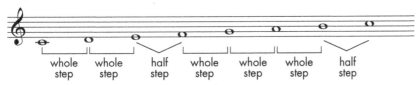

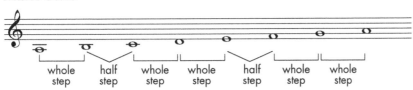

If the whole steps and half steps are lined up a little differently, we end up with a more melancholy sound known as a minor scale.

Minor Scale

Now listen to the singer in Track 59 sing the English folksong "Rue." Notice that the minor key makes a melancholy effect. Sing along with the accompaniment on Track 60, taking care to match the mood of the piece with your interpretation. This English folksong sports a play on words: thyme refers to time; rue refers to regret, as opposed to the shrub of the same name. The song is a gentle warning to beware of roguish men.

Rue

English Folksong

Copyright © 2000 by HAL LEONARD CORPORATION
International Copyright Secured   All Rights Reserved

Come, all you fair and ten - der girls that flour - ish in your
And when your thyme is past and gone, he'll care no more for
A wom - an is a branch - ed tree and man a sing - ing

prime, __ prime. Be - ware, be - ware, make your gar - den __ fair, let no man steal __ your
you. _____ And ev - 'ry day that your gar - den is waste will spread all o - ver with
wind. _____ And from her branch - es __ care - less - ly he'll take what he _____ can

thyme, _____ thyme. ⎫
rue, _____ rue. ⎬ Let ___ no man ___ steal _____ your _____ thyme.
find, _____ find. ⎭

MODES

Rules are meant to be broken, and so it is with key signatures. Sometimes major and minor scales simply don't have enough color and flavor to express what the composer wants to say. In that case, he or she may use a mode, which is a scale that's neither major nor minor.

Listen to the singer in Track 61 sing "Hava Nagila," paying attention to the accidentals in the printed music. Notice the slightly exotic sound of the mode. The mode, called Ahava Raba, takes the E minor scale and raises the fifth note—here, a D♯.

Hava Nagila

Copyright © 2000 by HAL LEONARD CORPORATION
International Copyright Secured All Rights Reserved

Traditional Hebrew

ROAD MAPS

When music repeats itself, or the composer wants sections of it to be restated, it's indicated through a system of shorthand symbols. This saves having to print additional pages of music that simply repeats something that has already happened.

Simple repeats are indicated with a repeat sign. If used singly, at the end of a piece or section, it indicates a return to the beginning of the piece or section. If used in a pair, like brackets, it indicates a repeat of the material between the two symbols.

Repeat Sign

First and Second Endings

Listen to the singers in Track 62 perform the blues ballad "Frankie and Johnny." Notice how the repeats work. Sing it yourself with the accompaniment in Track 63.

Frankie and Johnny

Copyright © 2000 by HAL LEONARD CORPORATION
International Copyright Secured All Rights Reserved

Anonymous Blues Ballad

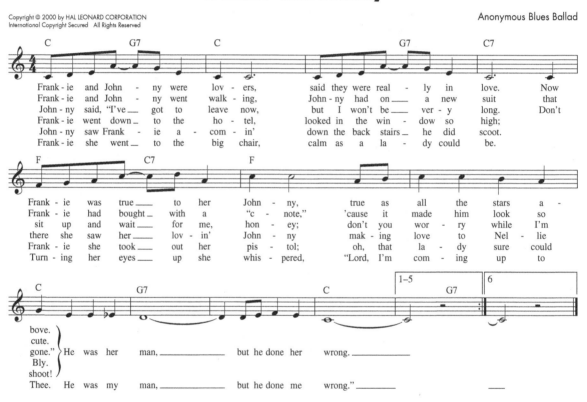

In addition to repeat signs, there are a few other signs used to indicate repeats of sections. *Dal Segno* is an Italian term meaning "the sign." It tells you to jump back in the music to the sign. It is followed by additional instructions.

Dal Segno

The other term you're likely to see is *Da Capo*. This Italian term means "the head," or "the top." Indicated in music with the abbreviation *D.C.*, or fully written out, the term tells the musician to return to the top, or beginning of the piece. It is often follow by another set of instructions:

D.C. al Fine: go the beginning and repeat the entire piece to the end.

D.C. al Coda: go to the beginning and continue to the *Coda* sign and then jump to the *Coda* section.

CHANGES IN KEY SIGNATURES

Now that you know where to look for a key signature, you should know that you have to keep your eyes open for changes in key signatures within pieces of music. Changing keys creates a colorful, interesting effect.

Look at "Luck Be a Lady" and notice the key changes. Look for a recording by Frank Sinatra and give it a listen. Notice that while the key change may look like a lurching change of gears, it's actually quite smooth and simple. Try singing along with the recording and notice how the harmony in the accompaniment makes it quite easy to sing through the key changes. "Luck Be a Lady" was written for the Frank Loesser musical *Guys and Dolls*.

Luck Be a Lady

from GUYS AND DOLLS

By FRANK LOESSER

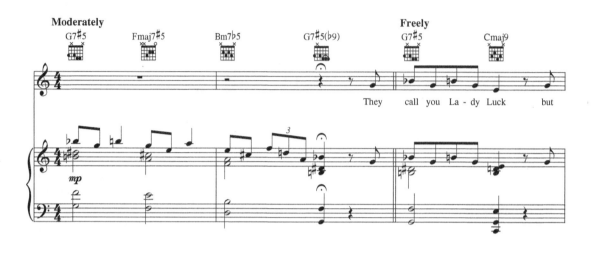

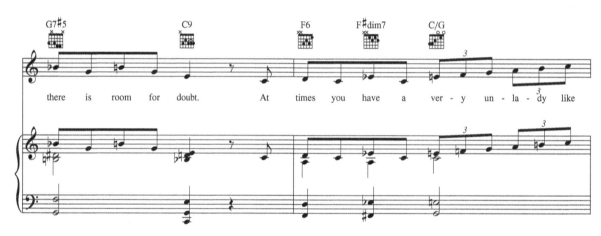

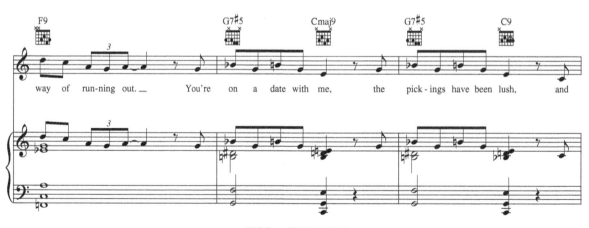

© 1950 (Renewed) FRANK MUSIC CORP.
All Rights Reserved

TRANSPOSING

It happens now and again that a song is simply too high or too low for a given singer to perform comfortably. In that case, singers have a choice of either not performing it all, or transposing it to a different key.

Listen to the singer in Track 64 Sing "One More Day" in the key of E. In Track 65, the song is sung in the key of D. In Track 66, the song is sung in the key of G. Try singing all three and see which key is the most comfortable for you.

One More Day

Copyright © 2000 by HAL LEONARD CORPORATION
International Copyright Secured All Rights Reserved

Sea Chantey

Oh, __ have you heard the news, my John - ny? One more __ day! We're home-ward bound to -
Oh, __ heave and sight the an - chor, John - ny, one more __ day! Oh heave and sight the
I'm __ bound a - way to leave you, John - ny, one more __ day! But I will not de -

mor - row, one more __ day!
an - chor, one more __ day! } On - ly one more day, my John - ny,
ceive __ you, one more __ day! }

one more __ day. Oh, rock and row me o - ver, one more __ day.

USING YOUR NEW SKILLS

Let's put some of your new music-reading skills to work. Written by Hughie Cannon and published in 1902, "Bill Bailey, Won't You Please Come Home" (often called just "Bill Bailey") is still popular with jazz bands and Dixieland bands. Listen to the singer on Track 67, then try it by yourself with just the piano part, on Track 68.

Look for recordings by the likes of Della Reese, Jimmy Durante and Ella Fitzgerald or Jimmy Durante and Ethel Merman.

Bill Bailey, Won't You Please Come Home

Words and Music by
HUGHIE CANNON

Copyright © 1995 by HAL LEONARD CORPORATION
International Copyright Secured   All Rights Reserved

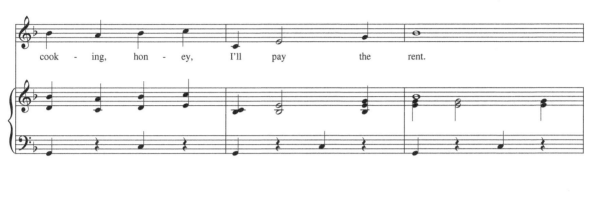

cook - ing, hon - ey, I'll pay the rent.

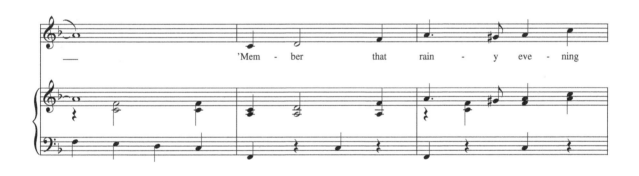

I know I've done you wrong.

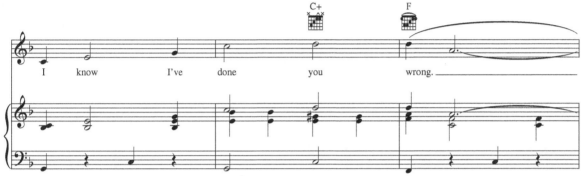

'Mem - ber that rain - y eve - ning

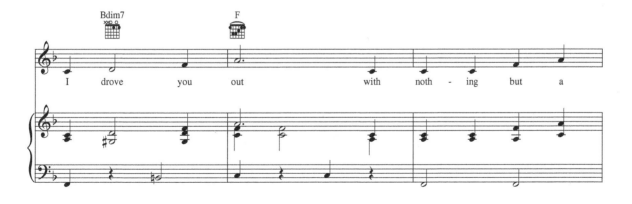

I drove you out with noth - ing but a

Also take a look at "Scarborough Fair." Most music fans know this old English folksong from recordings and performances by Paul Simon and Art Garfunkel. Listen to their take on the song and pay attention to how much impact an arrangement can have on a song. This is a handy song to know, whether you're singing around a campfire or performing at a wedding.

> Keep your eyes on the music to watch for such things as accidentals, key changes, time signature changes, repeats, and the like. Not all of these things will appear in every song you sing, but you should always be on the alert for such instructions.

Listen to the singer perform a few verses on Track 69. Try singing along to the accompaniment on Track 70. Have fun with this song—make it your own!

Scarborough Fair

Traditional English

1. Are you go - ing to Scar - bor - ough Fair?
2. Have {him}{her} make me a cam - bric shirt,
3. Have {him}{her} wash it in yon - der dry well,
4.-6. *(See additional lyrics)*

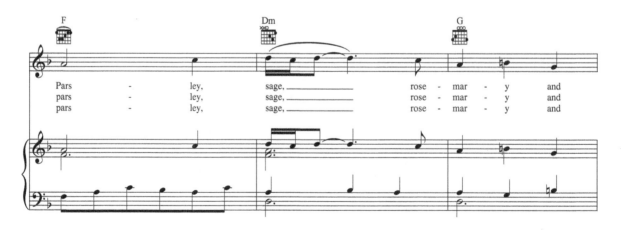

Pars - ley, sage, _____ rose - mar - y and
pars - ley, sage, _____ rose - mar - y and
pars - ley, sage, _____ rose - mar - y and

Copyright © 2009 by HAL LEONARD CORPORATION
International Copyright Secured   All Rights Reserved

Additional Lyrics

4. Have him (her) find me an acre of land,
   Parsley, sage, rosemary and thyme.
   Between the sea and over the sand,
   And then he'll (she'll) be a true love of mine.

5. Plow the land with the horn of a lamb,
   Parsley, sage, rosemary and thyme.
   Then sow some seeds from north of the dam,
   And then he'll (she'll) be a true love of mine.

6. If he (she) tells me he (she) can't I'll reply:
   Parsley, sage, rosemary and thyme.
   Let me know that at least he (she) will try,
   And then he'll (she'll) be a true love of mine.

Songs

"Hey Jude" is a Beatles anthem that grew out of a song Paul McCartney wrote for Julian Lennon at the time of his parents' divorce. John Lennon and McCartney are both credited with the song's final version. The Beatles recorded and released the song in 1968 with the song "Revolution" on the B-side. There have been a few covers over the years, by artists such as Elvis Presley and Wilson Pickett, but to sing this song you really must know the original.

"Memory" (don't confuse this song with "Memories," which is also worth singing) was written by Andrew Lloyd Webber for his hit musical *Cats*. It is based on T.S. Eliot's *Old Possum's Book of Practical Cats*. The song is sung by an aging glamour cat as she is about to end one of her nine lives to begin another. Look for recordings by Betty Buckley (Broadway) or Elaine Paige (West End), both of whom gave definitive performances of Grizabella and brought audiences to tears with this song.

"Rock Around the Clock" is a musical testament to the foolhardiness of the notion that rock and roll was a mere fad. Bill Haley and His Comets released their seminal recording of the song in 1955. It was not the first rock and roll recording, but it was the one that became an anthem for a generation of teens looking for a means of expression. It hit No. 1 on the U.S. and U.K. charts in '55 and has never left popular culture. It is heard in the soundtrack to the 1973 film *American Graffiti* and became the theme song for the television series *Happy Days*. As you work on the song and make your musical decisions, remember that Bill Haley's version is now etched into the minds of several generations of listeners. Expect your audience to sing along in this one!

"Single Ladies (Put a Ring on It)" can be sung with attitude or as a spoof—it's your decision. Watch Beyoncé's performance of the song, which was released in 2008, for a look at a performance with attitude. There is no shortage of spoof videos out there to inform your decision. Have fun with the song, no matter which approach you decide to take.

"What I Did for Love" was written by Marvin Hamlisch with lyrics Edward Kleban for the musical *A Chorus Line*. The show opened off Broadway in 1975 and moved to Broadway that same year, where it won Tony Awards for Best Musical, Best Book, and Best Score, along with a Pulitzer Prize for Best Drama. The show is set on a bare stage during auditions for a musical. Auditioners are asked, "If today were the day you had to stop dancing, how would you feel?" This song is a dancer's response. Look for a recording of Priscilla Lopez in the original Broadway cast recording, a lovely recording by Caroline O'Connor, or a very different take on the song by Grace Jones.

Hey Jude

Words and Music by JOHN LENNON
and PAUL McCARTNEY

Slowly

Hey Jude,_____ don't make it bad; take a
_____ don't make it bad; take a

sad song_____ and make it bet - ter._____ Re -
sad song_____ and make it bet - ter._____ Re -

mem - ber to let her in - to your heart; then you can start___
mem - ber to let her un - der your skin, then you be - gin___

To Coda

Copyright © 1968 Sony/ATV Music Publishing LLC
Copyright Renewed
All Rights Administered by Sony/ATV Music Publishing LLC, 8 Music Square West, Nashville, TN 37203
International Copyright Secured   All Rights Reserved

Memory
from CATS

Music by ANDREW LLOYD WEBBER
Text by TREVOR NUNN after T.S. ELIOT

Mid - night. _____ Not a sound from the pave - ment. _____ Has the moon lost her
Mem - ory _____ all a - lone in the moon - light _____ I can smile at the

mem - ory? _____ She is smil - ing a - lone. _____ In the
old days, _____ I was beau - ti - ful then. _____ I re -

Music Copyright © 1981 Andrew Lloyd Webber licensed to The Really Useful Group Ltd.
Text Copyright © 1981 Trevor Nunn and Set Copyrights Ltd.
All Rights in the text Controlled by Faber and Faber Ltd. and Administered for the United States and Canada by R&H Music Co.
International Copyright Secured   All Rights Reserved

Burnt out ends of smo-ky days,____ the stale cold smell ____ of

Rock Around the Clock

Words and Music by MAX C. FREEDMAN
and JIMMY DeKNIGHT

Copyright © 1953 Myers Music Inc. and Capano Music
Copyright Renewed 1981
All Rights on behalf of Myers Music Inc. Administered by Sony/ATV Music Publishing LLC, 8 Music Square West, Nashville, TN 37203
International Copyright Secured   All Rights Reserved

Single Ladies
(Put a Ring on It)

Words and Music by BEYONCÉ KNOWLES,
THADDIS HARRIS, CHRISTOPHER STEWART
and TERIUS NASH

Moderate groove

© 2008 EMI APRIL MUSIC INC., B-DAY PUBLISHING, SONY/ATV MUSIC PUBLISHING LLC, SUGA WUGA MUSIC, SONGS OF PEER, LTD.,
MARCH NINTH MUSIC, WB MUSIC CORP. and 2082 MUSIC PUBLISHING
All Rights for B-DAY PUBLISHING Controlled and Administered by EMI APRIL MUSIC INC.
All Rights for SONY/ATV MUSIC PUBLISHING LLC and SUGA WUGA MUSIC Administered by SONY/ATV MUSIC PUBLISHING LLC, 8 Music Square West, Nashville, TN 37203
All Rights for MARCH NINTH MUSIC Administered by SONGS OF PEER, LTD.
All Rights for 2082 MUSIC PUBLISHING Controlled and Administered by WB MUSIC CORP.
All Rights Reserved   International Copyright Secured   Used by Permission

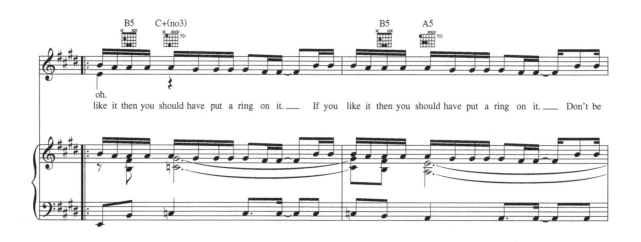

What I Did for Love

from A CHORUS LINE

Music by MARVIN HAMLISCH
Lyric by EDWARD KLEBAN

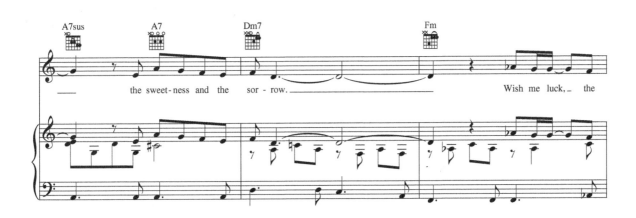

© 1975 (Renewed) EDWARD KLEBAN and SONY/ATV MUSIC PUBLISHING LLC
All Rights for EDWARD KLEBAN Controlled by WREN MUSIC CO.
All Rights for SONY/ATV MUSIC PUBLISHING LLC Administered by SONY/ATV MUSIC PUBLISHING LLC, 8 Music Square West, Nashville, TN 37203
All Rights Reserved

GLOSSARY

A cappella: An Italian term that translates as "in the chapel" or "in the church style." It refers to vocal or choral music that is sung without instrumental accompaniment. Barbershop quartets sing *a cappella*.

Accelerando: To grow gradually faster. Often abbreviated *accel*.

Accent: A small symbol placed over or under individual notes indicating that they are to be attacked with added weight or stress.

Accidental: A sharp, flat, or natural that is not indicated in the key signature and therefore has to be indicated specially in the music. An accidental appears as a sharp, flat, natural, double sharp, or double flat sign placed just before the note it affects. The accidental is cancelled automatically at the end of the measure in which it occurs, or by another accidental on the same note in the same measure.

Flat   Sharp   Natural

Double sharp   Double flat

Adagio: Tempo indication—an Italian term meaning "slowly."

Air: A term that originated in France and England in the 16th century that means "tune" or "song."

Allegro: Tempo indication—an Italian term meaning "quick and lively."

Andante: Tempo indication—an Italian term meaning "at a walking tempo."

Aria: The Italian word for song. Individual vocal numbers in an opera are called arias.

Art Song: A serious song, as opposed to a folksong, usually written for solo voice and piano. Such songs are not part of staged works like operas or oratorios; they are usually settings of poetry, and are intended for the recital stage.

Belting: A type of loud, powerful singing common in musical theater and some pop genres. When belting, a singer uses their chest voice in a higher-than-normal range to create a strident, distinctive sound that is similar to a musical yell. Although some singers belt throughout long careers, it can be dangerous to vocal health and has been known to end careers.

Bridge: The section of a song that alerts the listener to the fact that there is a change coming. It may precede the return of the song's opening melody, or it may precede the shift from the verse to the chorus.

Cabaret: This French word translates as "small room." It originally referred to little cafés and clubs, where patrons were seated at small tables. The form of entertainment that was born in these little clubs, a mix of song and dance, theater and comedy, also came to be known as cabaret during the 20th century. Today it often refers to intimate performance spaces, where patrons are seated at tables where beverages, and possibly food, are served during the performance.

Chart: Printed music—a slang term common among jazz musicians.

Chanson: Although this French word translates simply as "song," it is used to refer to a specific style of French-language songs. The songs, which put tremendous emphasis on delivery of lyrics, are generally sung in the *cabaret* style of the mid-20th century. The term *chanson* is also used in early music, where it refers to certain French songs of the Middle Ages and Renaissance.

Chest voice: Usually the speaking range of a singer, the chest voice is a singer's lower range, in which sung pitches resonate in the chest cavity. Both men and women have chest voices.

Clef: The symbol at the beginning of a line of music that tells the musician whether the staff indicates notes above or below middle C. The two most common clefs are *treble* and *bass*.

Treble Clef

E F G A B C D E F

Bass Clef

G A B C D E F G A

Coda: The final section of a piece of music.

Coda

Common Time: A shorthand time signature symbol indicating 4/4 time.

Con brio: Tempo indication—an Italian term meaning "with vigor."

Crescendo: To grow in volume, or get gradually louder.

Da Capo: This Italian term means "the head," or "the top." Indicated in music with the abbreviation D.C., or fully written out, the term tells the musician to return to the top, or beginning of the piece. It is often follow by another set of instructions.

> **D.C. al Fine:** go the beginning and repeat the entire piece to the end (Fine, pronounced "FEE-nay").

> **D.C. al Coda:** go to the beginning and continue to the Coda sign (Θ) and then jump to the Coda section.

Dal segno: This Italian term means "from the sign." It tells you to jump back in the music to the sign (segno, pronounced "SEH-nyoh"). It is followed by additional instructions.

> **D.S. al Fine:** go to the sign and then continue from there to the end of the piece.

> **D.S. al Coda:** go to the sign and continue from there to the Coda (Θ) sign and jump from there to the Coda section.

> Dal segno (the sign) 𝄋

Diaphragm: This is the sheet of muscle beneath your lungs that allows you to breathe and therefore allows you to sing. If you place your hand flat on your stomach, covering your navel, and shout "Ha!" as loudly as you can, you will feel your diaphragm do its magic. Singers use the diaphragm to support their vocal sound by creating a steady, even stream of air as they sing.

Diminuendo: To diminish in volume, or grow softer; sometimes abbreviated *dim.* or *dimin.*

Diva: This Italian word translates into English as "goddess," and is used to denote a great opera singer. In recent years it has been applied to any popular female singer as well as to any "high-maintenance" woman.

Dynamics: Levels of volume employed throughout a piece of music.

pianissimo – very soft	*pp*
piano – soft	*p*
mezzo piano – moderately soft	*mp*
mezzo forte – moderately loud	*mf*
forte – loud	*f*
fortissimo – very loud	*ff*

Early Music: Classical music written in Europe during the Middle Ages, Renaissance, and Baroque eras.

Espressivo: Interpretive indication—an Italian term meaning "with great feeling" or "expressively."

Fake Book: This is a very real book, often hundreds of pages long, that contains a collection of lead sheets—melody lines with guitar/keyboard chords written above them. Fake books often contain just one genre, like rock music or folk music.

Falsetto: A vocal technique in which men sing much higher than their natural vocal range. Typically only men and boys going through puberty have falsetto ranges.

Flat: The flat symbol (♭) lowers a note by one half step. A note that is out of tune because it sounds too low is also said to be flat.

Grace Note: A type of musical ornament in which one or more notes are added to a melody. On the printed page, the notes are smaller than the notes they ornament and are usually connected to the primary notes by a small slur.

Grand Staff: A staff in which the treble and bass lines are combined. This may be found in piano music or in music written for multiple voices, such as the four-part harmony of choral music.

Great American Songbook: A term used to refer to the large number of songs of Tin Pan Alley and the musicals of Broadway and Hollywood that were written and popularized between about 1920–1960. These songs are also referred to as "jazz standards."

Head Voice (or **head register**): The high range in which singers feel as though their sound is resonating in their head. Both men and women have head voices.

Improvise: To create a melody or harmony in performance.

Jazz Standard: A song from what has been called the "golden age" of American songwriting—the years between about 1920 and 1960. Such songs are also referred to as the "Great American Songbook."

Karaoke: A form of entertainment that originated in Japan in the 1970s. It features recorded music from which vocal parts have been removed, or at least minimized. Amateur singers are able to sing along with these "background" recordings, using a microphone and sound system. Karaoke is popular in clubs and bars around the world today. Simplified home systems are also available.

Lead Sheet: A sheet of music containing the melody and chord symbols to a piece of pop music. This is the type of music jazz players tend to prefer using, since the song is reduced to its essence, without anyone's arrangement getting in the way of their interpretation and improvisation.

Ledger Lines: Short lines that extend the musical staff.

Legato: An interpretive indicator—an Italian term meaning "smoothly."

Legit: Short for legitimate, although the full word is never used. Legit singers are those who sing without a microphone. They are also often called classical singers. A recitalist, someone singing a solo with a large chorus, or an opera singer would be "legit" singers.

Lento: A tempo indicator—an Italian term meaning "slowly."

Lieder: The German word for "song." In classical music it refers to art songs with German lyrics.

Major Scale (Key): Eight notes arranged stepwise in a rising or falling pattern so that the whole steps and half steps fall as follows:

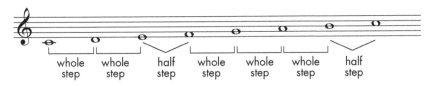

Measures: divisions within a line of printed music.

Minor Scale (Key): Eight notes arranged stepwise in a rising or falling pattern so that the whole steps and half steps fall as follows:

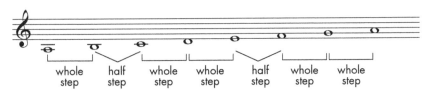

Moderato: A tempo indicator—an Italian term meaning "moderately."

Musical Theater: Very similar to operetta, musical theater is the term we usually apply to the Broadway musical. Musical theater productions can be comedies (*The Producers*), tragedies (*Blood Brothers*), or somewhere in between (*Rent*). Some musical theater productions are turned into films (*Chicago* and *Evita*) and some are based on successful films (*The Full Monty*).

New Music: Contemporary classical music, often defined as classical music, or art music, written since 1975.

Nodes/nodules: A singer's nightmare, a node or nodule is a growth on the vocal cords. They form where the cords touch to make sound, as the body's way of protecting the cords from damage—in much the same way that you get a callus on your finger. Nodes are usually preceded by hoarseness, a sign of irritation and inflammation of the vocal cords. Nodes can be caused by singing with a great deal of stress in the throat, screaming and shouting, singing outside your comfortable range, and even just falling into tense speaking habits. Careful, relaxed warm-ups, solid vocal technique, and taking care of your voice when you're not singing can help prevent nodes. If you are having some problems with hoarseness, see a doctor for diagnosis and care. To prevent them from occurring again, work with a good voice teacher.

Opera: A dramatic presentation, complete with sets, costumes and a pit full of musicians, in which the entire plot is sung. An opera that is costumed and set in a particularly opulent fashion, usually with dozens of cast and chorus members, is known as "grand opera."

Operetta: The Italian word means "small opera." The music and plots of operettas are lighter that those of opera and grand opera. Operettas are often frothy—even silly—productions, built around implausibly comical plot twists. The operettas of Gilbert and Sullivan (the English team of W.S. Gilbert and Arthur Sullivan) are among the most popular of the genre.

Oratorio: A musical piece featuring orchestra, vocal soloists, and chorus that tells a story. Unlike an opera, an oratorio is performed without scenery, props, or costumes.

Presto: A tempo indicator—an Italian term meaning "very quickly."

Prima donna: This Italian term for "first lady" comes from the opera world, where it originally referred to the leading lady, or female star, of an opera. In more recent years, the term has come to mean a woman who is difficult and arrogant.

Recitative: A section found in operas or oratorios in which the singer is accompanied by simple chords while delivering lines similar in cadence to normal speech.

Repeat: A symbol that tells the musician to go back and repeat a section of music. If used singly, at the end of a piece or section, it indicates a return to the beginning of the piece or section. If used in a pair, like brackets, it indicates a repeat of the material between the two symbols.

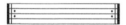

Sometimes repeat signs involve a first ending and second ending. The first ending is used the first time through the music, while the second ending is used the second time through.

Rests: Symbols that appear in music to indicate a specific interval of silence.

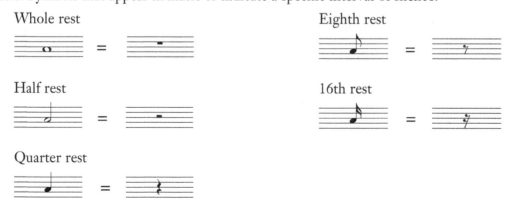

Ritardando: A tempo indicator—an Italian term meaning "holding back" or "becoming slower."

Scat singing: A type of improvisational jazz singing that is done either without words or with free-flowing, nonsense syllables ("Skoobie-doobie-dootn-doo-wah").

Sforzando: A strong, sudden accent. *sfz*

Sharp: The sharp symbol (♯) raises a note by one half step. A note that is out of tune because it sounds too high is also said to be sharp.

Sheet Music: This can be a confusing term, since it simply means printed music. The term was used at one time to differentiate recorded music from printed music. Even if you are singing a song that is found in a 600-page fake book, you are still singing sheet music.

Simile: Musical shorthand that indicates whatever interpretive marks occurred in the previous measure or measures should continue.

Sitzprobe: A German word that literally means "sitting rehearsal." This is the first read-through with the orchestra of the music of a musical, opera, or operetta—without acting, costumes, scenery, or props. The singers are usually downstage in front of the curtain, and the orchestra and conductor are in the orchestra pit.

Slur: A curved line extending over several notes in a piece of music indicating that they are to be performed without breaks or gaps between them.

Staccato: Small dots placed above individual notes that indicate they are be played short and detached.

Staff: The set of five lines on which music is written. (plural: staves)

Tempo: This Italian word—that translates to "time" in English—refers to the speed of a piece of music. Tempo is often indicated by a word, such as "allegro" or "adagio," or can be indicated with a metronome marking. ♩ = **120**

Tenuto: An Italian term meaning "bound" or "obligated." It indicates that a note should be held its full value. ♩ ♩̄

Throat Singing: A harsh-sounding style of singing heard among indigenous peoples from various parts of the world, including Eurasia, South Africa, and the far northern regions of North America.

Tie: A curved line connecting two or more of the same note, indicating that they are to be added together and sung as one, unbroken note.

Time Signature: A pair of numbers placed at the beginning of a song (after the clef and key signature), or in the course of a song, to indicate the meter of the music. The top number indicates how many beats will occur in each measure. The bottom number indicates what kind of note will get the beat.

4/4 time indicates four quarter-note beats per measure.

3/4 time indicates three quarter-notes beats per measure.

Tin Pan Alley: A term for writers and publishers of American popular music, specifically those in New York City from late 1800s to c. 1920. See also: Great American Songbook and Jazz Standard.

Transposition: Changing the key of a piece by moving it up or down in pitch.

Vamp: A repeating melody or accompaniment used in musical theater, jazz, and other styles.

Vibrato: A regular, even pulsation of pitch. Vibrato is used by singers and instrumentalists as an expressive tool.

Vivace: A tempo indicator—an Italian term meaning "quick and lively."

Yodeling: A style of singing or calling that requires switching quickly and distinctly from chest voice to head voice.

CD TRACK LISTING

Chapter 1: Finding Your Voice

1 matching pitches (female)
2 matching pitches (male)
3 singing scales (female)
4 singing scales (male)
5 "Sometimes I Feel Like a Motherless Child" (low key)
6 "Sometimes I Feel Like a Motherless Child" (high key)

Chapter 2: How the Voice Works

7 moving from chest voice into head voice (female)
8 moving from chest voice into head voice (male)
9 "Amazing Grace" (low key)
10 "Amazing Grace" (high key)
11 "Amazing Grace" (slower)
12 "Amazing Grace" (slower still)

Chapter 3: Breathing and Posture

13 "O Waly, Waly" (performance)
14 "O Waly, Waly" (accompaniment)
15 "Rockin' Robin" (accompaniment)
16 "My Heart Will Go On" (performance)
17 "My Heart Will Go On" (accompaniment)

Chapter 4: Daily Warm-Up and Practice

18 Vocal Warm-Up No. 1
19 Vocal Warm-Up No. 2

Chapter 6: Working on Your Songs

20 "Minstrel Boy" (performance)
21 "Minstrel Boy" (accompaniment)

Chapter 7: Making Music

22 "Shenandoah" (without expression)
23 "Shenandoah" (with shorter phrases)
24 "Shenandoah" (with longer phrases and cresc/dim)
25 "Shenandoah" (accompaniment)
26 "Your Cheatin' Heart" (performance)
27 "Your Cheatin' Heart" (accompaniment)

Chapter 8: Diction

28 "I fight fire."
29 "Sighing. Crying. Dying."
30 "Russian Lullaby" (performance)
31 "Russian Lullaby" (accompaniment)
32 "'O sole mio" (spoken text)
33 "'O sole mio" (performance)
34 "'O sole mio" (accompaniment)

Chapter 15: Getting Started

35 steady beat (metronome)
36 Counting Exercise No. 1
37 Counting Exercise No. 2
38 "Hey Lolly, Lolly" (sung using note names)
39 "Hey Lolly, Lolly" (sung using beat names)
40 "Hey Lolly, Lolly" (sung with the lyrics)
41 "Hey Lolly, Lolly" (accompaniment)

Chapter 16: You've Got Rhythm

Chapter 17: Keys, Scales, and Forms

Songs

female singer	Beth Mulkerron
male singer	Adam Estes
pianist	Teresa Drews
recording engineer	Ric Probst
producer	J. Mark Baker

ABOUT THE AUTHOR

Arts writer **Elaine Schmidt** is the author of *Hey Mom! Listen to This!: A Parent's Guide to Music*. She is a regular contributor to the *Milwaukee Journal Sentinel* and has written for *Current Musicology, Back Stage, Opera Canada, Music Express, American Record Guide,* and *Dance Teacher* magazines. Trained as a flutist and singer and holding an M.A. in Music Criticism, she has worked on nearly one hundred publications for Hal Leonard Corporation, G. Schirmer, and Ricordi and has scripted and hosted arts broadcasts on Milwaukee Public Television. She lives near Milwaukee, Wisconsin.

Pro Vocal® Series
SONGBOOK & SOUND-ALIKE CD
SING 8 GREAT SONGS
WITH A PROFESSIONAL BAND

Whether you're a karaoke singer or an auditioning professional, the Pro Vocal® series is for you! Unlike most karaoke packs, each book in the Pro Vocal Series contains the lyrics, melody, and chord symbols for eight hit songs. The CD contains demos for listening, and separate backing tracks so you can sing along. The CD is playable on any CD player, but it is also enhanced so PC and Mac computer users can adjust the recording to any pitch without changing the tempo! Perfect for home rehearsal, parties, auditions, corporate events, and gigs without a backup band.

WOMEN'S EDITIONS

MEN'S EDITIONS

MIXED EDITIONS
These editions feature songs for both male and female voices.

FOR MORE INFORMATION, SEE YOUR LOCAL MUSIC DEALER,
OR WRITE TO:

HAL•LEONARD®
CORPORATION
7777 W. BLUEMOUND RD. P.O. BOX 13819 MILWAUKEE, WI 53213

Visit Hal Leonard online at www.halleonard.com

Prices, contents, & availability subject to change without notice.
Disney charaters and artwork © Disney Enterprises, Inc.

0910

THE SINGER'S MUSICAL THEATRE ANTHOLOGY
THE WORLD'S MOST TRUSTED SOURCE FOR GREAT THEATRE LITERATURE FOR SINGING ACTORS
Compiled and Edited by Richard Walters

The songs in this series are vocal essentials from classic and contemporary shows – ideal for the auditioning, practicing or performing vocalist. Each of the eighteen books contains songs chosen because of their appropriateness to that particular voice type. All selections are in their authentic form, excerpted from the original vocal scores. Each volume features notes about the shows and songs. There is no duplication between volumes.

    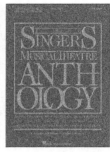 

VOLUME 1

SOPRANO
(REVISED EDITION)
00000483	Book/CDs Pack	$39.95
00361071	Book Only	$19.99
00740227	2 Accompaniment CDs	$22.99

MEZZO-SOPRANO/BELTER
(REVISED EDITION)
00000484	Book/CDs Pack	$39.99
00361072	Book Only	$19.99
00740230	2 Accompaniment CDs	$22.99

TENOR
(REVISED EDITION)
00000485	Book/CDs Pack	$39.95
00361073	Book Only	$19.99
00740233	2 Accompaniment CDs	$22.95

BARITONE/BASS
(REVISED EDITION)
00000486	Book/CDs Pack	$39.99
00361074	Book Only	$19.99
00740236	2 Accompaniment CDs	$22.95

DUETS
00000487	Book/CDs Pack	$39.95
00361075	Book Only	$18.99
00740239	2 Accompaniment CDs	$22.95

VOLUME 2

SOPRANO
(REVISED EDITION)
00000488	Book/CDs Pack	$39.99
00747066	Book Only	$19.99
00740228	2 Accompaniment CDs	$22.95

MEZZO-SOPRANO/BELTER
(REVISED EDITION)
00000489	Book/CDs Pack	$39.99
00747031	Book Only	$19.99
00740231	2 Accompaniment CDs	$22.99

TENOR
00000490	Book/CDs Pack	$39.95
00747032	Book Only	$19.99
00740234	2 Accompaniment CDs	$22.95

BARITONE/BASS
00000491	Book/CDs Pack	$39.95
00747033	Book Only	$19.99
00740237	2 Accompaniment CDs	$22.95

DUETS
00000492	Book/CDs Pack	$39.99
00740331	Book Only	$19.99
00740240	2 Accompaniment CDs	$22.95

VOLUME 3

SOPRANO
00000493	Book/CDs Pack	$39.99
00740122	Book Only	$19.99
00740229	2 Accompaniment CDs	$22.99

MEZZO SOPRANO/BELTER
00000494	Book/CDs Pack	$39.99
00740123	Book Only	$19.99
00740232	2 Accompaniment CDs	$22.95

TENOR
00000495	Book/CDs Pack	$39.95
00740124	Book Only	$19.99
00740235	2 Accompaniment CDs	$22.95

BARITONE/BASS
00000496	Book/CDs Pack	$39.95
00740125	Book Only	$19.99
00740238	2 Accompaniment CDs	$22.95

VOLUME 4

SOPRANO
00000497	Book/CDs Pack	$39.95
00000393	Book Only	$19.99
00000397	2 Accompaniment CDs	$22.95

MEZZO SOPRANO/BELTER
00000498	Book/CDs Pack	$39.95
00000394	Book Only	$19.99
00000398	2 Accompaniment CDs	$22.95

TENOR
00000499	Book/CDs Pack	$39.95
00000395	Book Only	$19.99
00000399	2 Accompaniment CDs	$22.95

BARITONE/BASS
00000799	Book/CDs Pack	$39.95
00000396	Book Only	$19.95
00000401	2 Accompaniment CDs	$22.95

FOR MORE INFORMATION,
SEE YOUR LOCAL MUSIC DEALER,
OR WRITE TO:

HAL•LEONARD®
CORPORATION
7777 W. BLUEMOUND RD. P.O. BOX 13819
MILWAUKEE, WISCONSIN 53213

VOLUME 5

SOPRANO
00001162	Book/CDs Pack	$39.99
00001151	Book	$19.99
00001157	2 Accompaniment CDs	$22.95

MEZZO-SOPRANO/BELTER
00001163	Book/CDs Pack	$39.99
00001152	Book	$19.99
00001158	2 Accompaniment CDs	$22.95

TENOR
00001164	Book/CDs Pack	$39.95
00001153	Book	$19.99
00001159	2 Accompaniment CDs	$22.95

BARITONE/BASS
00001165	Book/CDs Pack	$39.95
00001154	Book	$19.95
00001160	2 Accompaniment CDs	$22.95

THE SINGER'S MUSICAL THEATRE ANTHOLOGY – "16-BAR" AUDITION
00230039	Soprano Edition	$19.99
00230040	Mezzo-Soprano Edition	$19.99
00230041	Tenor Edition	$19.99
00230042	Baritone/Bass Edition	$19.99

TEEN'S EDITION

SOPRANO
00230047	Book/CDs Pack	$39.99
00230043	Book Only	$19.99
00230051	2 Accompaniment CDs	$22.99

MEZZO-SOPRANO/ALTO/BELTER
00230048	Book/CDs Pack	$39.99
00230044	Book Only	$19.99
00230052	2 Accompaniment CDs	$22.99

TENOR
00230049	Book/CDs Pack	$39.99
00230045	Book Only	$19.99
00230053	2 Accompaniment CDs	$22.99

BARITONE/BASS
00230050	Book/CDs Pack	$39.99
00230046	Book Only	$19.99
00230054	2 Accompaniment CDs	$22.99

*Prices, contents, and availability
are subject to change without notice.*

Please visit **www.halleonard.com**
for complete contents listings.

ORIGINAL KEYS FOR SINGERS

ACROSS THE UNIVERSE
Because • Blackbird • Hey Jude • Let It Be • Revolution • Something • and more.
00307010 Vocal Transcriptions with Piano $19.95

LOUIS ARMSTRONG
Dream a Little Dream of Me • Hello, Dolly! • Mack the Knife • Makin' Whoopee! • Mame • St. Louis Blues • What a Wonderful World • Zip-A-Dee-Doo-Dah • and more.
00307029 Vocal Transcriptions with Piano $19.99

MARIAH CAREY
Always Be My Baby • Dreamlover • Emotions • Heartbreaker • Hero • I Don't Wanna Cry • Love Takes Time • Loverboy • One Sweet Day • Vision of Love • We Belong Together • and more.
00306835 Vocal Transcriptions with Piano $19.95

PATSY CLINE
Always • Blue Moon of Kentucky • Crazy • Faded Love • I Fall to Pieces • Just a Closer Walk with Thee • Sweet Dreams • more. Also includes a biography.
00740072 Vocal Transcriptions with Piano $15.99

ELLA FITZGERALD
A-tisket, A-tasket • But Not for Me • Easy to Love • Embraceable You • The Lady Is a Tramp • Misty • Oh, Lady Be Good! • Satin Doll • Stompin' at the Savoy • Take the "A" Train • and more. Includes a biography and discography.
00740252 Vocal Transcriptions with Piano $16.95

JOSH GROBAN
Alejate • Awake • Believe • February Song • In Her Eyes • Now or Never • O Holy Night • Per Te • The Prayer • To Where You Are • Un Amore Per Sempre • Un Dia Llegara • You Are Loved (Don't Give Up) • You Raise Me Up • You're Still You • and more.
00306969 Vocal Transcriptions with Piano $19.99

GREAT FEMALE SINGERS
Cry Me a River (Ella Fitzgerald) • Crazy (Patsy Cline) • Fever (Peggy Lee) • How Deep Is the Ocean (How High Is the Sky) (Billie Holiday) • Little Girl Blue (Nina Simone) • Tenderly (Rosemary Clooney) • and more.
00307132 Vocal Transcriptions with Piano $19.99

GREAT MALE SINGERS
Can't Help Falling in Love (Elvis Presley) • Georgia on My Mind (Ray Charles) • I've Got the World on a String (Frank Sinatra) • Mona Lisa (Nat King Cole) • Ol' Man River (Paul Robeson) • What a Wonderful World (Louis Armstrong) • and more.
00307133 Vocal Transcriptions with Piano $19.95

BILLIE HOLIDAY
TRANSCRIBED FROM HISTORIC RECORDINGS
Billie's Blues (I Love My Man) • Body and Soul • Crazy He Calls Me • Easy Living • A Fine Romance • God Bless' the Child • Lover, Come Back to Me • Miss Brown to You • Strange Fruit • The Very Thought of You • and more.
00740140 Vocal Transcriptions with Piano $16.95

NANCY LAMOTT
Autumn Leaves • Downtown • I Have Dreamed • It Might as Well Be Spring • Moon River • Skylark • That Old Black Magic • and more.
00306995 Vocal Transcriptions with Piano $19.99

LEONA LEWIS – SPIRIT
Better in Time • Bleeding Love • The First Time Ever I Saw Your Face • Here I Am • Homeless • I Will Be • I'm You • Whatever It Takes • Yesterday • and more.
00307007 Vocal Transcriptions with Piano $17.95

THE BETTE MIDLER SONGBOOK
Boogie Woogie Bugle Boy • Friends • From a Distance • The Glory of Love • The Rose • Some People's Lives • Stay with Me • Stuff like That There • Ukulele Lady • The Wind Beneath My Wings • and more, plus a fantastic bio and photos.
00307067 Vocal Transcriptions with Piano $19.99

THE BEST OF LIZA MINNELLI
And All That Jazz • Cabaret • Losing My Mind • Maybe This Time • Me and My Baby • Theme from "New York, New York" • Ring Them Bells • Sara Lee • Say Liza (Liza with a Z) • Shine It On • Sing Happy • The Singer • Taking a Chance on Love.
00306928 Vocal Transcriptions with Piano $19.99

FRANK SINATRA – MORE OF HIS BEST
Almost like Being in Love • Cheek to Cheek • The Days of Wine and Roses • Fly Me to the Moon • I Could Write a Book • In the Wee Small Hours of the Morning • It Might as Well Be Spring • Luck Be a Lady • Old Devil Moon • Somebody Loves Me • When the World Was Young • and more.
00307081 Vocal Transcriptions with Piano $19.99

THE VERY BEST OF FRANK SINATRA
Come Fly with Me • I've Got You Under My Skin • It Was a Very Good Year • My Way • Night and Day • Summer Wind • The Way You Look Tonight • You Make Me Feel So Young • and more. Includes biography.
00306753 Vocal Transcriptions with Piano $19.95

STEVE TYRELL – BACK TO BACHARACH
Alfie • Always Something There to Remind Me • Close to You • I Say a Little Prayer • The Look of Love • Raindrops Keep Fallin' on My Head • This Guy's in Love with You • Walk on By • and more.
00307024 Vocal Transcriptions with Piano $16.99

THE BEST OF STEVE TYRELL
Ain't Misbehavin' • Fly Me to the Moon (In Other Words) • Give Me the Simple Life • I Concentrate on You • I've Got a Crush on You • In the Wee Small Hours of the Morning • Isn't It Romantic? • A Kiss to Build a Dream On • Stardust • The Way You Look Tonight • What a Little Moonlight Can Do • You'd Be So Nice to Come Home To • and more.
00307027 Vocal Transcriptions with Piano $16.99

SARAH VAUGHAN
Black Coffee • If You Could See Me Now • It Might as Well Be Spring • My Funny Valentine • The Nearness of You • A Night in Tunisia • Perdido • September Song • Tenderly • and more.
00306558 Vocal Transcriptions with Piano $17.95

ANDY WILLIAMS – CHRISTMAS COLLECTION
Blue Christmas • The Christmas Song (Chestnuts Roasting on an Open Fire) • Do You Hear What I Hear • Happy Holiday • Kay Thompson's Jingle Bells • The Little Drummer Boy • The Most Wonderful Time of the Year • O Holy Night • Sleigh Ride • What Are You Doing New Year's Eve? • and more. Includes a great bio!
00307158 Vocal Transcriptions with Piano $17.99

ANDY WILLIAMS
Can't Get Used to Losing You • The Days of Wine and Roses • The Hawaiian Wedding Song (Ke Kali Nei Au) • The Impossible Dream • Moon River • More • The Most Wonderful Time of the Year • Red Roses for a Blue Lady • Speak Softly, Love • A Time for Us • Where Do I Begin • and more.
00307160 Vocal Transcriptions with Piano $17.99

FOR MORE INFORMATION, SEE YOUR LOCAL MUSIC DEALER
OR WRITE TO:

HAL•LEONARD® CORPORATION
7777 W. BLUEMOUND RD. P.O. BOX 13819 MILWAUKEE, WI 53213

www.halleonard.com
Prices, contents, and availability subject to change without notice.

0411